A Guide to the Writing Workshop, K-2

Lucy Calkins

Photography by Peter Cunningham and André Martins

HEINEMANN ■ PORTSMOUTH, NH

This book is dedicated to Mary Ann Mustac, my closest partner, guide, and supporter for many years. Mary Ann, there aren't enough words to thank you for it all. I'm forever grateful. —LUCY

Heinemann • 145 Maplewood Ave., Suite 300 • Portsmouth, NH 03801 • www.heinemann.com

Offices and agents throughout the world

© 2023 by The Reading and Writing Project Network, LLC

The author and publisher wish to thank those who have generously given permission to reprint borrowed material:

THE RING BEARER. Text and Illustrations from THE RING BEARER by Floyd Cooper, copyright © 2017 by Floyd Cooper. Used by permission of Philomel, an imprint of Penguin Young Readers Group, a division of Penguin Random House LLC. All rights reserved.

THE KING OF KINDERGARTEN. Illustrations by Vanessa Brantley-Newton, copyright © 2019 by Vanessa Brantley-Newton; and text copyright © 2019 by Derrick Barnes. Used by permission of Nancy Paulsen Books, an imprint of Penguin Young Readers Group, a division of Penguin Random House LLC. and by permission of Scallywag Press, Ltd., London (UK title KING OF THE CLASSROOM). All rights reserved.

Yasmin the Chef, copyright © 2019 by Saadia Faruqi, illustrations copyright © 2019 by Picture Window Books. All rights reserved. Used with permission of Capstone.

Splash! Discover Sea Turtles by Virginia Loh-Hagan. Used with permission from Cherry Lake Publishing Group © 2016.

Saturday, by Oge Mora copyright © 2019 by Oge Mora. Cover illustration copyright © 2019 by Oge Mora. Little Brown & Company. Reprinted by permission of Little, Brown and Company, an imprint of Hachette Book Group, Inc.

HAIR LOVE. Illustrations, by Vashti Harrison, copyright © 2019 by Vashti Harrison; and text copyright © 2019 by Matthew A. Cherry. Used by permission of Kokila, an imprint of Penguin Young Readers, a division of Penguin Random House LLC. All rights reserved.

Insects Are Awesome by Michael Rae Grant. Copyright © 2023 by Heinemann and The Reading and Writing Project Network, LLC. Used by permission.

When Lunch Fights Back by Rebecca L. Johnson. Text copyright © 2015 by Rebecca L. Johnson. Reprinted with the permission of Millbrook Press, a division of Lerner Publishing Group, Inc. All rights reserved. No part of this text excerpt may be used or reproduced in any manner whatsoever without the prior written permission of Lerner Publishing Group, Inc.

Cataloging-in-Publication data is on file with the Library of Congress.

ISBN-13: 978-0-325-12854-2

EDITORS: Jessica Chadbourne, Natalie Chapman, Anna Cockerille, Dana Dillon, Havilah Jespersen, Zoë Kashner, Jean C. Lawler, Katherine Love Miller, Jennifer McKenna, Julia Mooney, Felicia O'Brien, Molly Picardi, Shannon Rigney, and Shannon Thorner

PRODUCTION: Rebecca Anderson, Carole Berg, Kerri Cardone, Kate Lennon, Vanessa Richards, Elizabeth Valway, and Richard Weed

COVER AND INTERIOR DESIGNS: Jenny Jensen Greenleaf

PHOTOGRAPHY: Peter Cunningham, André Martins, Nadine Baldasare, Elizabeth Franco, and David Stirling

ILLUSTRATIONS: Marjorie Martinelli

COMPOSITION: Publishers' Design and Production Services, Inc.

MANUFACTURING: Gerard Clancy

Printed in the United States of America on acid-free paper
1 2 3 4 5 6 7 8 9 10   MP   29 28 27 26 25 24 23

February 2023 printing / PO# 4500866375

CONTENTS

Works Cited are available in the online resources.

ACKNOWLEDGMENTS

This book is the very last to be completed, and as I write it, I'm full of reflections about the entire experience of revising the K–2 writing series. I am ever so grateful to all who have made this possible. This was no ordinary revision process. First, although we began this work well before the pandemic, the writing process mostly occurred during the months in which many of us had been holed away from the world. That allowed us to work with single-minded resolve, pouring our energy and imagination into an effort to do right by you and by kids. We've thought of this as our gift to the world. Every inch of the original series has been reconsidered and mostly rewritten.

I've had intense and brilliant help. My thanks go especially to Kate Montgomery, who has been my editor and writing partner for decades, and was my writing partner for the original Units of Study series. Kate turned to other work for a few years, devoting herself to international education and especially to the cause of refugees. When I began this effort, she recognized the importance of it and joined me at the helm. She's helped me to imagine ways this series can live up to its potential, and she's helped me rally, guide, and support coauthors and to get the books written.

A few others have been writing partners throughout. I especially thank Katie Clements and Valerie Geschwind. These colleagues, like Kate, poured their imagination, teaching talent, wisdom, and zeal into this project.

The team at Heinemann has been equally all-in. Our team has benefited from inspired leadership by Jessica Wollman. A few of our many editors have been especially helpful to me. I thank Anna Cockerille, who has been a partner for many years. This work is in her bones: she can write, lead, and teach with brilliance. I've also been blessed with guidance from the talented Zoë Kashner, Natalie Chapman, and Felicia Rothman. Carole Berg has effectively led the production team, doing so despite all the pandemic challenges and TCRWP's tendency to constantly revise. I appreciate her ability to lead her team so the job gets done on time, and with stunning results. Thank you to Elizabeth Valway, who was the production editor on this *Guide* and who has dedicated her production talents to our portfolio for many, many years. Jenny Jensen Greenleaf, our graphic designer, is another long-standing partner. Thank you, Jenny, for your stunning work on this entire series and in particular on this *Guide,* which took special consideration and vision.

Lisa Bingen pours heart and soul into marketing. We can finish each other's sentences, and that teamwork has wrought marketing miracles. Ashley Puffer supports

Lisa and the overall marketing effort in ways that inform and educate the field about what we have to offer.

All of my work at TCRWP is supported by a few key people. For decades now, Mary Ann Mustac has been my close friend and ever-present partner, helping me to balance my roles as organizational leader, professor, teacher, writer, and human being. She brings finesse, warmth, and wisdom to her work. Janet Steinberg has been a courageous critic and guide, making the series far more data-based and aligned to standards. Thank you also to equity reviewers from within and outside our organization: Lorena Lopez, Aeriale Johnson, Connie Pertuz-Meza, and Tiana Silvas-Brunetti. Amanda Hartman has lifted the level of all our K–2 teaching. Emily Butler Smith and Beth Neville make the organization of TCRWP work for all of us. Laurie Pessah and Mary Ehrenworth join me at the helm of the project, helping us be a family that learns together. Both Mary and Laurie help me and our organization listen to our colleagues and to teachers, school leaders, and kids, responding with great care and with imagination. They also keep me believing that this work is worth living for.

Finally, I whisper a prayer of thanks to my parents and my spouse, each of whom died while this effort was underway. Thanks to Evan and Virginia Calkins and to John Skorpen. How glad I am that I continue to have eight siblings, three kids (Kira Spinner, Miles Skorpen, and Evan Skorpen), thirty-one nieces and nephews, lots of glorious graduate students, and a grand family at Teachers College and at the Teachers College Reading and Writing Project.

Series Overview

Series Overview

Welcome, friends, teachers everywhere. I'm thrilled you are here, opening the very first pages of our newly revised curriculum, Units of Study in Writing, K–2. I hope this set of books becomes a companion and a comfort for you and that it draws you into the larger community of practice that surrounds these units and the Teachers College Reading and Writing Project (TCRWP). Most of all, I hope that these resources help you support the young people in your care on their journey toward becoming more confident, engaged, and expert writers who use literacy to live joyfully, to regard their own lives as significant, and to work as curious, empathetic, and involved citizens of the world. And I hope the Units of Study inspire you to give your writing workshop the blood, sweat, and tears it deserves.

In this resource, you'll find four units of study for each grade level that fit tongue-in-groove alongside each other, each accounting for about five weeks of teaching. Each new unit in the sequence helps students consolidate, use, and build upon what they have already learned. There will also be freestanding out-of-the-box units that can be inserted into your curricular sequence. The combined sequence of units will comprise the heart and soul of your writing curriculum, and we expect they will travel back and forth between school and home with you as you annotate them and use them in your teaching. All told, your grade-level Units of Study in Writing kit provides you with:

- **Four Units of Study.** Each of the four units offers a sequenced set of daily sessions that invite students along a path of writing development in one of three genres: narrative, information or explanation, and opinion or argument writing. Each daily session includes:

  ▸ An **essential teaching point** that encapsulates a technique or strategy that writers can use repeatedly when they generate ideas for writing or plan, draft, revise, or edit their writing.

- **The words and methods we use to explain, demonstrate, and engage children** in learning to use that day's teaching point. Reading these, you can imagine you are watching my coauthors and me as we teach the lesson that you'll soon teach. We share scripts of our teaching in the hope that you learn from and adapt our example.

- **Suggestions for ensuring access** to the work of the day—making it accessible in ways other than those detailed in the session.

- Along the margins of the lesson, in italics, **notes about the teaching**—tips for modifications, explanations for choices we've made, cautionary bits of counsel, and particular **support for multilingual language learners** (MLLs) and for digital writing.

- Each session has been previewed in Spanish on a video. Charts have been translated into Spanish and there are suggested mentor texts in Spanish.

- **High-leverage small groups and one-to-one conferences** you are apt to lead that day and all-important tools you can use to support the work of the day, the unit, and writing development.

- **Anchor charts and one-day charts** that can be printed as student-sized charts. These will travel across the units with students and be carried between home and school. These charts will help you support kids' progress along a trajectory of writing development.

- **Additional Resources.** In addition to the units themselves, your resources include:

  - This volume, *A Guide to the Writing Workshop, K–2.* This guide serves as an overview of the essentials of a writing workshop, helps you with all-important methods, introduces practical management tips, and guides you to lead your writing workshop.

  - *Supporting All Writers: High-Leverage Small Groups and Conferences, K–2.* This book supplements your units, providing you (and resource teachers) with easy access to ready-to-teach small groups and conferences around major writing goals. It includes work times that especially support children who are either below or above benchmark, ensuring that all children progress along a trajectory of development.

  - *Writing Pathways: Performance Assessments and Learning Progressions, K–2.* This resource contains the assessment system for the K–2 Units of Study in Writing. In it, you'll find a chapter that provides an overview of writing development, plus assessments, checklists, exemplar texts, and annotated benchmark pieces of writing, at each level for all three genres.

  - **Access to online resources.** The online resources provide you with downloadable versions of charts, handouts, book lists, exemplar texts, and more, all arranged session by session to streamline each day's preparation for you. As new research comes out, and as the community of practice at TCRWP develops new insights, we regularly release updated information into these online resources. 👏

The Relationship between Units of Study and Professional Development

TCRWP is the world's preeminent provider of professional development in writing. In this series, we've drawn on all we know about providing state-of-the-art professional development so that the units double as both curricular support and professional development. Our fondest dream would be for every teacher using these units to have the opportunity to work with a TCRWP staff developer, watching us and coteaching this curriculum and then meeting afterward to discuss and reflect on the reasons behind decisions and to imagine and weigh alternate ways the instruction could have gone. Because providing that professional development in person to every school isn't possible, we've tried to design this series to be a next-best alternative.

As you read through the units, you'll see how my colleagues and I would teach each unit. In the "Unit Essentials" section, the coaching text, and this guide, we explain decisions we've made. We do not expect you to follow our teaching exactly; we provide the details you'll see so that you can understand not only broad outlines for how a unit might unfold, but also the ways we suggest you interact with children. The end goal is not the teaching that we describe here, but the teaching that you and your children invent together.

Grounded in a Research Base

The series is written to represent coherent and abiding research-based principles. You  can look at any day's teaching at any grade level, K–8, and see the same underlying beliefs in operation. The methods you use, whether you are leading a minilesson, teaching a small group, conferring, or assessing a writer, have all been piloted, revised, improved upon, and refined across decades—and the logic that informs all this teaching is explained in sections of this guide devoted to each of those methods.

For example, your teaching will always follow David Pearson's "gradual release of responsibility" model, which, in brief, can be described as "I do, we do, you do" (Pearson and Gallagher 1983). Your students first learn from your demonstration (accompanied by an explicit explanation), then from engaging in guided practice in which the amount of scaffolding they receive is lessened over time, and then from independent work, on which they receive feedback. Then, too, your conferring and small-group work with writers will be informed by John Hattie's (2008) research on the feedback that accelerates learners' progress. To give feedback, you watch youngsters and study their writing to see the new work they have tried. You celebrate something the learner has done that you hope the learner will do again, often. Then you decide on, demonstrate, and explain next steps the learner can take. As students try those next steps, you watch attentively, noting their progress, and learning from instances when your teaching hasn't yielded results, and adapting that teaching in hopes of making a palpable difference.

Making This Work Your Own

Because you'll use just a few teaching methods every day in your teaching of writing, you and your colleagues will find that as you teach with the support of the units, you are actually refining those methods and becoming stronger in using them. As you teach (and learn by teaching), you'll be well positioned to support and learn from each other: if one teacher is especially effective at leading small groups, colleagues across the entire school can benefit from observing and emulating her small-group instruction. And because the methods that you use to teach writing are also critical to effective instruction in reading and in math, the professional development that you engage in within your writing workshop will have important ramifications for all your teaching, making you a more deliberate, strategic, and effective teacher across your day.

How are the new units similar to and different from the previous version of these units?

This series represents a wholesale revision. The best of the previous Units of Study has been streamlined, clarified, and kept, but the new units are new indeed. These are some of the guiding principles behind the innovations:

- This version of Units of Study is **more culturally relevant, accessible, affirmative, and engaging** for all learners. The teaching builds students' identities, helping them value and tap into their lived knowledge. We hope that all children see themselves in the examples we provide and the teaching we give. We include a video preview in Spanish for each session and have translated teaching points and charts into Spanish. There are also blue coaching notes in the margins of each unit book specifically designed to help support your MLLs. Most of the mentor texts are by diverse authors. Every session includes an "Ensuring Access" section, aimed at making the unit as inclusive as possible.

- We've provided **more support for students to transfer their phonics knowledge into the writing workshop** and also for them to **develop their phonics and phonological awareness skills** through writing. The emphasis on writing conventionally has increased, including a new focus on editing and punctuation.

- The sessions are **shorter and livelier.** They contain more songs, more dramatic play, more opportunities to pretend. They are as richly developmental as possible.

- The **units fit much more tongue-in-groove together**. We are careful to make sure instruction reinforces and extends prior learning. Often charts—say, a chart of ways to work with partners—are used across a sequence of units. We are more apt to remind kids (and ourselves) of what they learned during the prior year, making sure that there is a clear trajectory not only in major skills but also in classroom management, partnership work, use of tools, and the like.

Instead of checklists, K–1 writers now use anchor charts to guide their formative assessments in each genre.

- The **assessments are far more child friendly and developmentally appropriate**. In the younger grades, children do not need to know when a particular day's writing time is setting them up to produce writing that you will assess. When children first begin assessing their work, they assess it against their familiar anchor chart—instead of using the checklists, which, at this point, are more useful as teacher tools for calibrating growth than as child-friendly tools.

- The **storyline of the units is much clearer**, and you'll communicate the storyline to your children so they know what unit they are in, even what the focus is of a particular bend in the unit. That is, everyone will realize that Bend I of the unit aims to do one thing, Bend II, something different. The storyline will be far clearer than it was in previous-edition units.

- The **work times are designed so you can open your unit and easily teach them**. Each day's session includes the small groups, conferences, and conferring tips your students are most likely to benefit from, along with irresistible charts and tools. A separate, responsive teaching book, titled *Supporting All Writers: High-Leverage Small Groups and Conferences, K–2*, pulls together the highest-leverage, most-engaging work times from across the curriculum and groups them into a series of easy-to-use progressions. This resource will be especially useful for meeting the range of needs in your classroom and for intervention.

- We've puzzled through why some concepts have been hard for kids to grasp and **invented new teaching to support tricky concepts**. For example, we have found new ways to help kids keep their Small Moment stories small. We've created lessons teaching young writers how to strategically use text features and illustrations to support their information writing. We've developed research clubs to help students of varying reading levels learn and write about topics together. We've created engaging opportunities for writers to use video and other multimedia techniques to share their opinions digitally.

- We **draw on the latest research on the science of reading and on knowledge generation**. We are more explicit about the ways that writing can support phonological awareness. We support kids in orthographically mapping words. In nonfiction books, especially those dealing with research, we help kids bring more prior knowledge to their work with a topic and emphasize the importance of learning and using key vocabulary, including webs of words.

The Authorship of This Series

Although the Units of Study books read as if one teacher created and taught the minilessons, mid-workshops, small groups, and shares, the creation and teaching are actually vastly more collaborative. Before we revised the new series or began work on any specific new unit, most of us at the Project will have worked for years to develop, teach, adapt, and refine the general outline of the unit or many components of it. These versions of the units benefit from the wisdom and experiences of the 75+ staff members at TCRWP and from decades of research and teaching.

Of course, during all that time, teachers, school leaders, and graduate students have been developing, teaching, extending, rethinking, and revising the units; so these units also bear the DNA of the teachers, principals, literacy coaches, and graduate students with whom we teach and learn.

Once the actual writing of this particular iteration of a unit begins, the coauthors and I pass the manuscript between us continually—sometimes doing so for a year. Researchers, writers, equity readers, editors, graduate students, and senior Project leaders also contribute to the manuscripts in process and review them after drafts are done to guide revisions. Master teachers pilot units as we write them, and their wisdom and their children's wisdom informs each unit as well.

All of this means that although the books read as if they draw on one classroom, depicting the story of how that unit of study unfolded in that classroom, in truth, the classroom depicted in these books is a composite classroom, and the kids' voices are captured or created from all the kids we've taught. And although only two or three names appear on the cover of a book, each unit stands on the shoulders of the TCRWP community and, therefore, has, in a sense, been coauthored by the entire staff of this organization and by the children, teachers, principals, superintendents, and researchers who have become part of this community of practice.

Questions & Answers

Q My kindergartners don't yet know their letters and sounds, nor have they been socialized into the behaviors that are expected in a writing workshop or even in school itself. Should I take a few weeks to acclimate them before we launch?

A This is a familiar concern. Please trust us when we tell you that we have carefully written the earliest units in kindergarten so they support kids before they know their letters and sounds, bringing them toward that knowledge. The units themselves will also teach kids the tools, patterns, and expectations of a writing workshop so you needn't dedicate time to socializing them. Please start teaching Unit 1 right away. But yes, it is vitally important that you teach phonics alongside the Units of Study in Writing, and know that the writing workshop will support your phonics instruction.

Q What are the all-important guidelines I need to keep in mind from the start?

A Most of the guidelines that are especially important now, as you orient yourself to the units, revolve around time. Your writing workshop will go worlds better if you teach it at least four times a week, giving at least forty-five minutes to it. Regard each session as a single day's workshop. You'll be tempted to spread some sessions across two days, but we advise against that. To teach units at this pace, it will be important for you to keep your minilessons lively and brief. Lean on Chapter 5 for support with that. Tightening your minilessons is key, because kids learn from their work more than from your talk, and they need time to do that work. Finally, it is important to plan on a unit lasting no more than five weeks.

Q What resources will I need to get started?

A There are only a few all-important things you need. First, each teacher needs his or her own copy of the Units of Study. Then, too, kids need access to lots of paper, and across the class, there should be a variety of paper. This is not a time to stint on paper. In the online resources for each grade, you'll find templates for paper that you can print. In almost every K–2 unit, we recommend that kids write in three- to five-page booklets. Also, kids need utensils for writing. In early kindergarten, markers are wonderful, and we recommend multicolored markers with colors representing many skin tones. Later in kindergarten, and in the other primary grades, pens are easier for kids than pencils. Finally, each unit relies on a small set of mentor texts. All the texts highlighted in the units are available in the trade pack accompanying the units. You do not need class sets of these texts—two or three copies suffice. Most of all, you need to teach in the company of others. I hope your school leaders have read *Leading Well: Building Schoolwide Excellence in Reading and Writing*, and I hope your grade-level colleagues are teaching this curriculum alongside you and that there is time set aside for you to plan together and to visit each other's classrooms.

You'll find the Facebook community, Units of Study in Writing, provides enormous support and gives you access to TCRWP. Finally, the online resources accompanying these units provide a deep well of materials to complement and support your teaching.

Closing Comments

The ensuing chapters are written in the order in which I hope you read them. First, you'll read about **workshop essentials:** the time devoted to writing, the direct instruction techniques, the mentor texts, the responsive feedback from a teacher, the collaboration and feedback from peers, and the writing process that will become familiar to your students. Next, you'll learn to put **first things first,** establishing the rituals and routines that support your students in being engaged and independent writers. Next, you'll read about **setting up your writing workshop,** how to use your classroom space, charts, writing supplies, and mentor texts to support your writers. After that, you'll read about the origin and purpose of **the minilesson,** which begins every writing workshop, and how to tailor your minilessons to best support your students. Then, you'll read about **conferring,** the heart of your teaching in a writing workshop, and the specific methods for productively working with students in this way that we've honed over the decades. You'll also learn how best to use **small groups** to support your students in creating a collaborative learning community. Next, you'll learn how to run a writing workshop where every day, you are **affirming and supporting English learners** and committed to **ensuring access** for all learners.

A team of educators, authors, and researchers created these units with the best and most up-to-date understanding of how children learn to write. However, you are the ultimate expert on how your particular children learn and what they need. Take this teaching into your classrooms and try the lessons as written, then work with colleagues to adjust as needed. Soon, you'll see that your effort and careful attention are rewarded. Not only will your students' writing soar to new heights, but your teaching will become more effective, more attuned to your students than ever before.

Essentials of the Writing Workshop

Essentials of the Writing Workshop

Writers need time to write.

Children need time to write. Granted, giving kids fifty minutes a day, every day, to write will not be easy. In the overcrowded hodgepodge curriculum of today, with everyone adding more and more things for you to squeeze into your day, it can be brutally hard to make time for children to write. Yet doing so is the single most important thing you can do for your kids as writers.

Everything important, meaningful, and beautiful takes time. Writers need time to generate ideas and content, to imagine how the text might go, to rehearse, to draft, to reread and rethink and revise, to learn from feedback, to edit. Children also need time to combat anxieties, to dare to take risks, to rise to the moment.

Building Writing Volume and Confidence

Designating time for a writing workshop is an important start, but it is also important that during that block of time, children actually produce lots of writing. Only when children get into the swing of producing lots of writing will their writing carry the sound of a human voice, will the writer elaborate, write with detail, and grow new insights through writing. Just as fluency matters to readers, being able to write with volume matters for writers. If writing feels like chiseling in marble for students—if it takes five minutes to write a single sentence—it is unlikely they'll develop their potential as writers. Learning to write, like learning to play baseball or to swim, only happens when the learner has lots of time to practice.

Giving Time to Writing Creates Dramatic Results

I can promise that if you prioritize writing, and if kids actually write during your writing time, then you'll see dramatic results. When my colleagues and I help school leaders visit writing classrooms to give teachers critical coaching, we show them that it is important to look beyond the published writing on the wall. They need to open up the writing folders to take into account the sheer amount of writing a student has done today, yesterday, the day before. When students date each day's writing and collect all their writing until the unit is complete, it is easy to track the volume of writing each student produces each day. By mid-year, first-graders generally write a three-page book almost every day, with four or five sentences on a page; that's four books a week. Second-graders are apt to write a five-page booklet across two days, with more like ten lines of writing on each page.

When a writing workshop is taught with passion and power, and when it is treated as a subject deserving of the same time that reading and math are given, then the writing workshop creates dramatic results. Children's writing soars—and the workshop invigorates your entire school day—creating intimacy between you and your students, between your students and each other, and altering the entire learning culture in your classroom.

Making Time for Writing: A Typical Schedule of a Workshop Classroom

There is no question that incorporating a writing workshop into your schedule will take purposeful planning. Each of you will need to design your schedule so that it is aligned to the school, district, and sometimes state standards and expectations, as well as to your values and your children's interests and needs. The schedule will be somewhat different in kindergarten, first grade, and second grade. As children grow older, disciplines such as social studies, science, and math will be given more time, and choice will be given less time.

Sample Schedule

	Time	Activity
	Prior to 8:30	Unpack, jobs
	8:30 – 8:45	Morning Meeting, Interactive Writing, and Phonemic Awareness
	8:45 – 9:45	Writing Workshop
	9:45 – 10:15	Choice Time
	10:15 – 10:35	Phonics
	10:35 – 10:45	Shared Reading with Phonics
	10:45 – 11:45	Reading Workshop
	11:45 – 12:20	Lunch and Recess
	12:20 – 1:00	Thematic Studies (science/social studies, may include interactive writing, shared reading, read-aloud, or writing)
	1:00 – 1:40	Special (Art, Music, Science)
	1:40 – 2:30	Math Workshop
	2:30 – 3:00	Read-Aloud and Book Talk

*At the beginning of the year when kids are building stamina, K–2 teachers can supplement reading and writing workshop periods with extra sessions of phonics, read-aloud, shared reading, and shared writing.

This sample schedule can be found in the online resources.

Writers need explicit instruction, shared writing wisdom.

Children not only need to write, they also need direct, explicit instruction in the skills and qualities of effective writing. We wouldn't consider turning down the lights and saying to math students, "Multiply!" Yet somehow, some people think it is okay to teach writing by turning on some music and saying, "Write," and then responding to whatever kids churn out by saying, "What a poet you are." We do students no favors by pretending that the writer within each child needs only to be unleashed. The truth is that instruction dramatically improves a child's writing. I can walk into a school, look at the writing on display, and know within a minute whether the kids are receiving explicit instruction in the qualities and strategies of good writing, because that instruction produces results—and not next year, but the next day, the next week. Children not only need to write, they need direct, explicit instruction in the skills and qualities of effective writing.

Let me show you what I mean with an example from a narrative writing unit in first grade. Early in the unit, children are given three-page booklets and encouraged to think of a small moment that they remember and to tell that moment across their fingers, then to sketch that moment across three pages of a booklet. Once they've sketched and said the story, they write it. Typically, early in the unit, the story is very bare bones. Let's pretend Leo's goes like this:

> I went to my brother's soccer game.
> I sat on the bench.
> He got the ball.
> I screamed and screamed.
> He made a goal. I was glad.

You can lift the level of Leo's story (and of every subsequent story he writes) by teaching him to story-tell and write in twin sentences. This means instead of saying, "I sat on the bench," and then moving on to whatever happened next, Leo would say and write another sentence—a twin sentence—about sitting on the bench. So he adds, "Lots of my friends sat there too."

Leo then can do that work with every subsequent sentence. "He got the ball" becomes, "He got the ball. He dribbled it to the goal."

The bigger point is that explicit instruction in writing matters, and when you teach a skill that is transferable to other texts, it matters for life.

Writers need the opportunity to learn from other writers and their texts.

Writers also benefit from models, from mentor texts. Imagine, for example, that you want to teach children how to write a How-To text. Think of the zillions of tips and lessons you'd need to give them to communicate instructive suggestions that could all be

conveyed simply by showing children an example of the sort of text you hope they'll write. The exemplar text could include ingredients and be organized as steps, with each additional part of the sequence accompanied by an instructive picture that has numbers and arrows to show action and sequence. Meanwhile, the sentences in the exemplar could also suggest time sequence, incorporating phrases such as *first* and *after that*.

Finding Mentors as a Lifelong Skill

When mentor texts and other models accompany your instruction, you are teaching children how they can, in the future, be their own writing teacher. You convey that whenever they want to write anything, they can find a text that represents the sort of thing they hope to write, and then closely study what that writer has done, asking, "What has this writer done that I could try as well?" Your instruction also becomes more multilevel, because writers can decide which texts and what aspects of the text they will emulate.

Another advantage of mentor texts is that they are concrete, physical, hands-on. Visit effective writing workshops and you'll see youngsters annotating a mentor text, perhaps with sticky notes, as they talk to a partner, saying, for example: "Look, he put talk into his story. I am going to try that in my story."

Mentor Authors Are Career Role Models

Mentor texts also help students see that people like them can become authors, and that the life experiences of people like them matter to readers. When your class gathers around texts written by authors with rich, varied backgrounds and experiences, you send an important message that affirms all of your children.

Some Favorite Mentor Texts

Grade K Unit 1

In an interview with *Heise Reads and Recommends*, Derrick Barnes speaks about how his youngest son, Nnamdi, begged his dad to put him on the cover of one of his books. When he was asked to write a book about preparing one of his sons for kindergarten, he said, "I thought about how many books had I actually seen based on a kid's experience with heading to kindergarten that featured an African-American boy—there were none. I was definitely the man to tell the story." After helping four sons prepare for kindergarten, Barnes had all the material he needed to write.

Grade 1 Unit 4

In an interview with *Book Riot*, Saadia Faruqi says, "I really wanted Yasmin to be a reflection of her readers: kids who may be South Asian, kids who may be first-generation American, and kids who may be Muslim. In fact, Yasmin is a reflection of childhood itself: she's curious and creative, but she also has self-doubt and gets bored or dejected easily."

Grade 2 Unit 2

Virginia Loh-Hagan writes both nonfiction and fiction for children, and also teaches at the university level. She writes with her audience in mind—students and teachers she remembers from the ten years she taught in an elementary school. "I write books that I would've used in my own classroom. I write books that I would've wanted to read as a young reader," she explained in an interview with author Justin Colón.

Teachers and Other Children Can Be Mentors Too

When providing children with mentor texts, it is helpful to remember the advice given by developmental psychologist Lev Vygotsky. Vygotsky (1978) pointed out that learners need instruction that is within their "zone of proximal development." To provide this to your students, seek out published texts that closely resemble those your students can write. Also, use examples written by children and write your own demonstration texts. For example, if many of your students have labeled their drawings with one-word labels, you might make a text in which you label your drawings with sentences, such as "this is a button," that include many high-frequency words. That text can be even more helpful if you add labels in front of the children, showing how you think: "Wait, how do I spell *the?* Hmm, . . ." and then head over to the word wall and study the spelling of the word, adding it to your label. That is, in writing workshops, kids learn from watching you work on demonstration texts.

Writers need a coherent, cumulative curriculum in writing, one that builds across kinds of writing and across grades.

One reason that schools today are adopting systemic, whole-district approaches to the teaching of writing is the widespread agreement that, just as teachers can't teach kids to multiply fractions unless children have first learned what fractions are, so, too, teachers can't teach higher-level writing skills unless kids come to you with prerequisite understandings. For third-grade writers to be able to write literary essays, it's helpful if they've already had repeated opportunities to write persuasive speeches, letters, and petitions, each including claims and supports, in first and second grade. For children to be able to write effective feature articles in fourth grade, it is helpful for them to have written structured All-About books prior to then.

Writing in the Context of Standards and Testing

Think of it this way. One would never dream of launching a child's entire *reading* education by giving that child a chapter book or text-prep materials to read. Yet somehow, there are schools that teach almost no writing at all until the kids face high-stakes tests. It's important to remember that, just as oak trees grow in the fullness of time, so, too, do writers. Your colleagues in upper elementary grades need to be able to count on your students coming into their classrooms with foundational skills in place.

Although some states have rejected the new iterations of the Common Core, substituting their own adaptations of those standards, the standards movement has nevertheless helped districts recognize the importance of a coherent writing curriculum that builds over time. The standards are not themselves a curriculum; they merely aim to answer the question, "How good is good enough?" But by providing a year-by-year answer to that question, the standards convey the message that kids need explicit instruction and opportunities to practice every year.

A Trajectory of Narrative Writing Development

Sixth-graders write with new attentiveness to a story arc. Their stories begin with a set-up in the beginning, then create rising tension in the middle, and reveal a change or resolution by the end. Students continue to add earlier or later scenes, doing so with increasing intentionality. They might add a flashback to build the problem or show why the character wants something or a later scene to show how the episode connects to a solution.

Fifth-graders ask, "What is it about this story that matters most?" and they move the timeline of their story to advance the story's deeper meaning. Students learn to make their characters travel through time and space, adding future or past events into their narratives, they revise to forward significance.

Fourth-graders learn to rehearse different ways a story might go prior to drafting. They try starting or ending their stories in different places on a timeline, and stretch out exciting parts or parts where the protagonist felt a big emotion. A major emphasis is on pacing, as fourth-graders learn to control how time moves across their stories.

Third-graders write with a story arc in mind. They learn to write stories that are similar to the ones they are reading, with many of their stories featuring several scenes that are each a small moment. First the trouble starts, then the trouble gets worse, and finally the trouble gets resolved.

Second-graders write Small Moment stories about one focused time in which the main character experienced a strong feeling. They ask, "What is the most important part?" and then can start and write their story right before that part. They use emojis or quick sketches to plan how feelings will change across their story. This is the beginning of work with a story arc.

First-graders write small moments where they tell the story of a thirty-minute or so chunk. They learn to differentiate between a watermelon story, one that contains a zillion seed stories, and a more focused seed idea. Later, first-graders transfer what they've learned to write Small Moment stories about fictional characters who do or want something. They work on their endings, creating satisfying endings by telling what happens to characters at the end.

Kindergartners learn to tell and write stories that go across pages, writing one part on each page. Then they learn to use "turn the page" words to connect what's happening between pages, words like *one night* and *then*. There's no expectation that kids will write focused stories.

Grade 6
Personal
Narrative

Grade 5
Turning
Life into
Literature

Grade 4
Spinning
True Stories
into Gold

Grade 3
Series
Fiction

Grade 2
Small
Moments

Grade 1
Small Moments
and Scenes
to Series

Grade K
Writing for
Readers

Special Issues for Schools New to the Workshop Model

If your classroom is full of children who have no experience with this curriculum, you need to consider how best to acclimate them to the workshop model and ready them for the demands of your grade level. This is more challenging in the older grades. Certainly, for example, Unit 1 of grade 2 will be a stretch for second-graders if they've never been in a writing workshop. I recommend you borrow a unit from your grade 1 colleagues and start the year with that unit. Any one of the first-grade units could be used as a ramp into second-grade work. You'll also borrow some sessions from earlier grades that your children seem to need. For example, if your second-graders are not spelling with independence, you might borrow sessions from kindergarten, such as "Spelling Words Bravely," from Bend I of Unit 2. You'll also want to draw on *Supporting All Writers: High-Leverage Small Groups and Conferences, K–2.*

You may also wonder if, as a teacher new to the Units of Study, there's a reason to teach the units in the order they are presented, or if it makes more sense to pick and choose based on other factors in your overall existing curriculum. Mostly I'd be hesitant to use the units out of order, especially with the first two units at a grade level. The units have been built sequentially, one upon the other. The teaching is cyclical; key teaching points are reintroduced across units and grade levels, each time with more complexity and in ways that expect more on the students' part. That said, once you and your colleagues are deeply familiar with the units, you certainly can swap the sequence of the final two units, as long as you know this will require revisions to the units.

Writers need responsive feedback—from you, their teacher, and from partners who support their next steps.

The writing workshop was once called the "conference approach to teaching writing" in recognition of the fact that one-to-one conferences are at the heart of your teaching. In *Learning by Teaching* (1982), Donald Murray, the man credited with inventing the writing-process approach to teaching writing, describes the importance of these conferences by saying:

> I am tired but it is a good tired, for my students have generated energy as well as absorbed it. I've learned something of what it is to be a childhood diabetic, to raise oxen, to work across from your father at 115 degrees in a steel drum factory, to be a welfare mother with three children, to build a bluebird trail . . . to bring your father home to die of cancer. I have been instructed in other lives, heard the voices of my students that they had not heard before, shared their satisfaction at solving the problems of writing with clarity and grace.

> I feel guilty when I do nothing but listen. I confess my fears to a colleague, Don Graves. He assures me I am a demanding teacher for I see more in my students than they see in themselves. . . . Teaching writing is a matter of faith—faith that my students have something to say and a language with which to say it.

Conferring Pinpoints Successes and Next Steps

John Hattie's research gives new clout to the importance of conferring. In his book, *Visible Learning* (2008), Hattie suggests that few things accelerate a learner's progress as much as effective feedback. Feedback, ideally, includes naming what the learner has done successfully, glowing especially over new efforts and breakthroughs—and then naming concrete, specific next steps the learner can take. When teaching writing, it is especially helpful if the feedback is transferable to other pieces of writing so that the writer learns something that will help another day with another piece.

For example, perhaps when writing a story, the writer's initial draft ends with a solution that seems to come out of nowhere. In a writing conference, instead of responding simply to the ending of that particular story, you might explain that anytime one writes a story, it's best to find a solution or resolution within the existing elements of the story so the solution doesn't seem to fly in out of nowhere, Superman style.

Writing Partners Have Each Other's Back

In writing workshops, writers share their work in progress with peers and the most important peer is the writer's partner. Partnerships matter because all of us learn best when someone has our back, when someone is rooting for us. The brass tacks of partnerships are relatively simple. You tend to choreograph these relationships, which remain intact for a unit of study (at least a month). Children typically sit near their partners, both during the minilesson and throughout writing time. Partners talk as they sit alongside each other, writing, although that gradually lessens in second grade. They especially talk during interludes that come in the middle and at the end of most writing times. You'll probably invite a writer's partner to listen in whenever you confer with the writer, because that gives you a way to teach the partner how to help the writer.

Although the essentials of partnerships can be quite simple, experienced writing workshop teachers are usually aware that these relationships deserve more atten-

tion than we often give them. Writing partnerships can bring together people of different genders, peer groups, races, classes, personalities. The opportunity to write with support from someone who is outside your own bubble of existence can be precious. As renowned social researcher Brené Brown explains, in life, we often protect ourselves against vulnerability, and yet in doing so, we protect ourselves from all that we most long for: intimacy, wholeheartedness, I-thou connections. When partners hear each other's stories and take the great risk of being open with each other, they come to trust each other, to cheer for each other.

When writers grow up within a culture of feedback and when they give feedback to each other often, they learn to give feedback to themselves. When you ask a youngster, "What do you think of your draft so far?" and "What are you planning to do next?" you are teaching that writer that those questions are worth asking of one's own writing. A child who grows up in a culture of feedback develops a deliberate metacognitive "other self" that allows that writer to shift between writing and rereading, drafting and revising.

Writers need opportunities to experience the writing process.

Units of Study in Writing stands on the shoulders of a giant body of research that began forty years ago when Don Graves and I conducted the first National Institute of Education study on how children develop as writers. That groundbreaking research led to, and was part of, what has been described as a revolution in the teaching of writing.

Essential Transformative Findings about Writing

- There is a process that writers use that is as foundational to writing as the scientific method is to science. Whether a writer is writing an editorial, a fantasy story, a poem, or a petition, that writer will rely upon the same process. That process can be described as including rehearsal, drafting, revision, and editing.

- Writers benefit from being taught how to use the process of writing. Writers benefit from being taught the recipe for effective stories, essays, petitions, and books.

- Even children as young as five can be taught the writing process that adult writers use. As Jerome Bruner (1960) once wrote, "The foundations of any subject may be taught to anybody at any age in some form."

Writing as a Process and Skill

It's important that kids grow up knowing they don't need to be geniuses to write. They just need a process that works for them, one that allows them to start with whatever thoughts, memories, information they have on hand and one that allows them to make something of that. As teachers, it's important to keep in mind that teaching youngsters the process of writing is not the same as teaching them the names of presidents. Children need to be at home with their own versions of the writing process so that, when they aspire to write something, they know what to do: how to start and what to do next

and next after that. For example, if a child is going to write an article about a favorite pizza parlor, she should know that she'll start by announcing that the place is great, and then she'll shift into telling why.

And it is important that kids know that just as they can get better at basketball by studying people who play that game and by working on their technique for foul shots, dribbling, and the rest, so too, they can get better at writing by studying people who write well. They can take on, practice, and become adept at strategies and techniques that those people use.

Writers need the opportunity to write for real audiences.

Publication is not a prize for writing, so much as it is a part of the process of writing. The reason our young people need to publish their writing, then, has everything to do with the fact that when we write for readers and for causes, it puts demands on our writing. A writer asks, "Will my friends be able to follow my recipe and make the cookies?" or "Will this letter end up bringing more books by kids like me to our classroom library?" Readying a piece for an audience, the writer asks, "How can I make readers, listeners, workers feel what I want them to feel?" and "Is this the best I can do? How can I do better?"

Audiences beyond the Classroom Are Meaningful

It's a beautiful thing when children's writing is mounted onto bulletin boards, but it is even more precious when writers are given the chance to reach real-world audiences. Writing is for books to be read, poems to be recited, songs to be sung, and letters to be mailed. When writers receive responses often enough that they internalize the idea that everything they write can have an audience, they are more apt to ask, "What effect will this text create?" "How can I spell so people can read my writing?" "How can I be certain these words will matter to readers?" Writing for readers is important. Having readers who sigh and laugh and remember and cry and wince and argue is what compels us to work with zeal and galvanizes a deeper kind of revision.

Parades, Parties, and More

When a unit of study ends, you'll always want a celebration. Usually, each child will have selected one piece to improve and "fancy up" for publication. It's fun to vary your celebrations across the year, often letting them become more elaborate as the year progresses—on the other hand, the first celebration of the year can also be particularly special. Many schools celebrate kindergartners' very first published book ever with a parade through every hallway of the school, with the entire school community lining the halls and cheering as kids chant, "Two, four, six, eight, our stories are really great. One, two, three, four, we can't wait to write some more!"

A K–2 Writing Process

Within a unit, kids move through the writing process multiple times, producing new writing (usually booklets) each time.

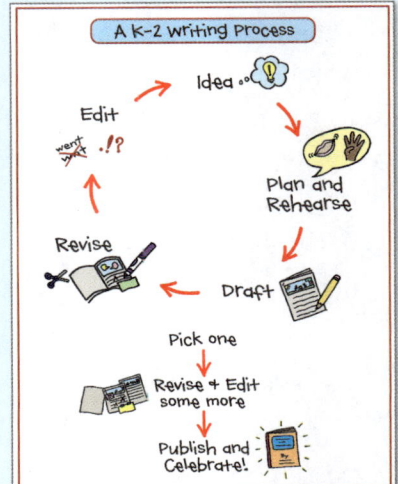

Idea: Writers start by thinking up an idea for what they'll write. They might use a strategy to help them: "Think of a person you love and remember a special time with that person."

Plan and Rehearse: Writers spend a few minutes planning and rehearsing how their piece will go, perhaps by touching the pages of a booklet, saying aloud what they plan to write, and then sketching each page.

Draft: Writers write their piece across the pages of a booklet.

Revise: Writers revise by adding new passages with revision flaps and strips. They can try new beginnings or new endings, can expand one line into a paragraph, can take a booklet and make it into two booklets, each with a clearer focus. Young writers can also reread their writing, imagine the questions that others will have, then use revision to respond to those imagined questions.

Edit: Writers fix up their writing to make sure it's ready for readers. They edit for spelling, capitalization, letter spacing, and punctuation, among other things.

After kids have moved through the writing process several times, filling a folder with pieces, they choose one piece to fancy up and publish.

Revise and Edit Some More: Writers choose the one piece they most want to share with the world. Mentor texts give them images of further next-step work, and they also use previously learned strategies to revise and edit even more (without recopying).

Publish and Celebrate: Writers might add color to their illustrations or make a special cover. Then, they share their writing with the world, sometimes by mailing it, wrapping it up as a gift, and often through a classroom publishing party with invited guests.

That celebration can be far simpler, however. The parade can be through the classroom, ending at the "We Are Authors" bulletin board. Then the bulletin board might be toasted with juice and celebrated with cookies. Later in the year, the classroom might be turned into a "museum," with children's work displayed on desks, full of sticky notes that say, "Ask me." The author sits near the work, ready to explain his strategies and decisions. The important thing is that these are lively and celebratory.

Avoid asking every child in your class to read his writing to the entire class, because that will drag on. Instead, channel children and visitors to sit in small groups and, in each group, one child after another can read aloud, with the listeners responding by chanting a refrain. Sometimes, they chime in on an adaptation of "Catch a falling star, put it in your pocket" and say, "Catch a fleeting moment, put it in your pocket, save it for a writing day." If published work can be word-processed by an adult, then a copy or two of each child's published piece becomes an important part of the class library, available for readers. When this happens, children will often read their own and one another's writing during the reading workshop.

First Things First
Center Your Teaching around Kids' Work

First Things First
Center Your Teaching around Kids' Work

Stephen Covey (1996), the great expert on leading for change, suggests that leaders need to prioritize, to put first things first. You, as a classroom teacher, are the leader of a complicated organization and yes, prioritizing is all-important. In teaching writing, your priority needs to be creating time, place, motivation, and momentum for youngsters to work with agency, independence, and zeal on their own writing projects. Because the minilesson comes first in your writing workshop, and so clearly requires your attention, it's easy to become overly focused on it. Don't overlook the truly all-important thing about a writing workshop—the opportunity for young children to work with deep engagement on writing projects they care about, drawing on their ever-growing knowledge of phonics, high-frequency words, and writing skills and strategies.

> *Writing workshop is a precious bubble of time.*

Katherine Bomer, a close colleague of ours and author of *A Teacher's Guide to Writing Workshop Essentials* (2020), describes the writing workshop as, "a precious bubble of time—an uncluttered, uninterrupted space for thinking, writing, and responding." I love that image. Consider approaching your workshop, intending to cordon it off from other parts of your day in ways that make it special, even revolutionary. And know that when your writing workshop works its magic, it will end up changing your whole day—and you—in the process.

Imagining a Writing Workshop in Which Youngsters Carry On with Independence

It helps if you can imagine how this will go, which can be a bit of a challenge when you are trying to imagine a class of 28 five-year-olds—kids who may not know their letters and sounds—writing with agency, independence, and zeal! In *Writing Pathways*, we detail what writing development looks like. Let's focus, for now, on the structures and systems that support this work.

Materials, Skills, and Tools at the Writer's Fingertips

Once things are up and going in your workshop, children will take their two-pocket folder from a box, which you'll probably color code to match their seating area. Inside the folder will be all the writing the child has done thus far within that particular unit of study. In one pocket will be the ongoing, unfinished writing. The child will pull her most recent piece from that pocket, select a writing utensil from a table caddy of writing tools, and begin by rereading what she wrote the preceding day, then adding on to that piece. When the child decides that her piece is completed (which will happen at least every other day), she simply moves that piece to the other pocket in the same folder. Then she chooses more paper and begins to write a new piece.

When early writers reread their ongoing work, they may be reading a text that doesn't contain words, so the rereading might essentially be storytelling. That is, this work is multilevel enough that all children can participate with some independence. To be able to carry on like this, there are things children need to know—things like strategies for coming up with topics and things to do if the writer feels stuck. Those, and a lot of other things, will be taught in your minilessons.

As mentioned earlier, the nature of children's work will be determined by the unit. In one unit, children will write poems; in another, persuasive letters and petitions, in another, nonfiction chapter books. You will often determine the genre and will sometimes ask all writers to work on a shared strategy. (For example, you might say, "Today, among all the other work you are doing on your nonfiction books, will you take a few minutes to add headings, text boxes, glossaries to, at least, your most current nonfiction book?") Remember, however, that children do not rely on the minilesson alone as the source of their work. For example, if a minilesson focuses on writing endings to a story or on making sure that when spelling, each syllable contains a vowel, children won't just work on their endings or their vowels! Instead, they'll rely on all they know to carry on as writers.

Avoid Bottlenecks by Affirming Writers' Decision Making

Even very young children need to "own" their own version of a writing process. That is, they need to be able to choose a topic, rehearse for writing, draft a piece, revise, and edit their writing, then start a new piece. The important thing for you to know is that with your permission or your help, your kids will progress through these parts of the writing process. You don't function as a gatekeeper. Because it's important to avoid bottlenecks, with kids lining up behind you to ask for directions so they can continue work, kids need to be able to move from one part of the writing process to another without your okay. You don't want children to need to secure your permission to get more paper, to figure out the spelling of an unfamiliar word, to use the stapler, to declare their piece finished, and so on. If you watch your teaching and your kids' work, and notice when bottlenecks occur, you can teach in ways that help children get past those bottlenecks.

> *Even very young children need to "own" their own version of the writing process.*

So, yes, kids can declare a piece of writing to be done and they can move on to the next piece. You may, in a conference, bring that "finished piece" back into play, but it's better for kids to move on than for them to sit, waiting for you. So this means that, yes, a child can get new paper for a new project. You'll want to teach children which kinds of paper will provide them with enough challenge, and from time to time you'll graduate them to new paper. Meanwhile, for some children, the cycle of writing—from choosing a topic to finishing a piece—might take one day, for others, two or even three days. This will be a longer process for more proficient writers, who will work on more substantial pieces and devote more time to rehearsal and revision.

Getting Started Every Day by Writing and Rereading

Because your 28 or more children will all be carrying on as writers, shifting from choosing a topic to drafting to revising , this means that on any one day, some kids will be drawing pictures and rehearsing, others will be in the midst of drafting, still others will be taking apart booklets to resequence their pages. Some, of course, will sit in their chair, waiting for you to provide them with an individualized jump start—which isn't the way you want things to go. You can make it less likely that children leave the minilesson and then just wait for you to come around if you teach them that the first thing writers do is to write their name on their paper (if this is a new piece of writing). If they are working on an ongoing piece, encourage them to start every day by rereading their writing. Writing one's name on the page and rereading the existing text are two ways to lure a writer toward the page. Drawing pictures serves the same function.

While very young children write, they talk companionably with each other—and to themselves. Most of the teachers I know seat writers at tables to encourage children to make running commentaries as they work. These side-by-side commentaries do a lot to make writing workshops into the richest sort of language workshop imaginable. Listening in, you might hear kids muttering things like this:

"My mom *feeds* baby mice. They are soooo cute!"
"How do you spell /ē/ like in happ*y?*"
"Bear, bear, that's a bear. Hey—that's funny: bare-bear! Bare-bear."
"Wait a minute. I got two *m*'s. Mmmmm!"
"Know what my puppy does? She bites her tail!" "Mine bites *me!*"
"Help! My *y* is banging my *a* on the head. Oops! Look out!"

Of course, when you encourage children to work companionably alongside one another, talking quietly as they work, this can spiral into too much talk and that becomes increasingly so as kids get older. By the second half of second grade, much of the talk is cordoned into specific talk times: conferences, mid-workshops, share sessions. One way to channel children toward quieter work is to designate times and places for them to talk. This will tend to be more applicable for second-graders, although midway through the year, some first-grade teachers also decide that their children are mature enough to benefit from silent writing time, punctuated with deliberately chosen intervals for talk. These teachers tend to institute whole-class "private writing times" and whole-class intervals for partnership talk.

Setting Up a Workshop that Allows Kids to Work with Independence and Engagement

It will be a challenge to establish the hum of an effective workshop. Lucille Clifton, a former U.S. Poet Laureate, has said, "Nurture your imagination of what's possible. You cannot create what you cannot imagine." I'm hoping this guide helps you to nurture your image of possibility, so that you approach your teaching of writing imagining a writing workshop that is magical. To inspire your dreams of what you and your students can achieve, you might watch videos of up-and-running workshops on the Units of Study in Writing Facebook page and the TCRWP website.

Managing the Classroom Environment

For a writing workshop to work well, it is characterized by ideas that are still pretty revolutionary in American education. Visit a state-of-the-art writing workshop and you will feel the difference as kids—even five- and six-year-olds—work with agency and initiative, making choices, deciding what to draw and write about, choosing when to staple and tape, when to progress from one story to another, when to read a draft to a friend, or when to walk over to the word wall.

In setting up your workshop, you are aiming to make a place where people can carry on, deeply invested in their own important projects, while you move among the students, coaching, demonstrating, channeling.

Successful Management Takes Skill and Time to Develop

Some people in the field of education act as if classroom management is a low-level focus. I can't help but point out that corporate management is an executive skill; high-level executives are often coached in ways to organize time, space, and personnel to maximize productivity. So don't fool yourself into thinking that managing your writing workshop won't take skill and effort. How could it *not* be tricky to build an environment in which twenty or thirty youngsters pursue their own important projects, all working within the confines of a small room, each needing his or her own mix of silence and collaboration, time and deadline, resources, and one another?

Yet the truth is that in effective writing workshops, teachers find ways to make it so that there aren't long lines of needy children, constant interruptions, and work that lasts for only brief stretches of time. I always encourage teachers who are new to writing workshops to visit an established writing workshop.

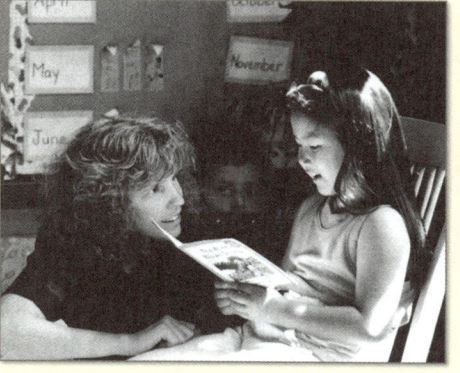

The following is from the first edition of *The Art of Teaching Writing* (1994):

I used to think that to teach creative writing I needed to have a creative management system. I thought creative environments, by definition, were ever changing, complex, and stimulating. Every day my classroom was different: one day we wrote for ten minutes, another day, not at all; sometimes students exchanged papers, and other days they turned them in; sometimes they published their writing, sometimes they didn't. My classroom was a whirlwind, a kaleidoscope, and I felt very creative. Rightly so. My days were full of planning, scheming, experimenting, and replanning. Meanwhile my children waited on my changing agendas. They could not develop their own rhythms and strategies because they were controlled by mine. They could not plan, because they never knew what tomorrow would hold. They could only wait.

I have finally realized that the most creative environments in our society are not the kaleidoscopic environments in which everything is always changing and complex. They are, instead, the predictable and consistent ones: the scholar's library, the researcher's laboratory, the artist's studio. Each of these environments is deliberately kept predictable and simple because the work at hand and the changing interactions around that work are so unpredictable and complex.

To teach writing, you need to establish an environment and structures that will last throughout every day of your teaching. The essential premise, one that undergirds any writing workshop, is this: the writing workshop needs to be simple and predictable enough that your youngsters can learn to carry on within it independently.

Because the work of writing is complex and varied, because students need to be able to follow their texts toward meaning, and because you need, above all, to be able to coach writers who are engaged in the ongoing work of writing, the writing workshop in most classrooms proceeds in a similar way through a similar schedule, using similar room arrangements and materials.

Being Present with Voiceovers, Students Shadowing You, and More

During work time, you will probably find it works best to move among children, talking with them at their workplaces, dotting the room with your presence. Every day, you can confer with a few children, lead several small groups and do some mid-workshop interruptions (through which you say something to the whole class).

You make your presence matter more by telling children that if they need you, instead of waiting in their seats (where they tend to cause trouble because they are just waiting), they may shadow you. That way, you keep kids who need your help close by, where they can benefit from your teaching. For most of a conference, you'll probably look intently into the face of the one child, ignoring the eavesdroppers in a way that spurs them to listen more intently. As your conference ends, turn to the others who've listened in, saying, "Do any of the rest of you want to try that too?"

Nurturing Independence in Every Writer

When children don't carry on productively in a writing workshop, it's important to take the time to diagnose the cause. Sometimes, the issue is not management, but inspiration. You might need to make a greater effort to cherish writing so that children want to put their stories and opinions and expertise onto the page. Then, too, sometimes trouble stems from children feeling that the work you expect is beyond their reach. If children don't regard writing as doable and worth doing, they will either act out or tune out. The *Supporting All Writers: High-Leverage Small Groups and Conferences, K–2* book provides particular support in these areas.

It's easy to be so busy rushing from one child to the next that you don't have time to stop and study the patterns in your class. How easy it is for me to sympathize with this because often I, too, am so busy running that I do not stop to ask, "Where am I going?" What each of us needs to remember is that the answer can't lie in our running faster and faster. There's got to be a better way, but you can only discover that way if you give yourself time to observe, to think, and to secure help by anticipating and planning for classroom management.

A Quick Check of Your Writing Workshop Routines

To assess your classroom routines, you might periodically assume the role of observer of your writing workshop, asking yourself questions such as:

1. How efficiently do children get up, push in their chairs, and come together in the meeting area?
2. How easily do children assemble the tools they need for writing?
3. How long can children work independently or with partners without needing redirection or prompts from me?
4. Am I able to lead a few small groups or conferences without the class becoming chaotic?
5. When a child finishes a piece of writing, does the child get started on a new piece?

Supporting Classroom Rituals and Routines across the Writing Workshop

⑥ Whole-Class Share

One Piece on the Outside

Students pack away their writing at the end of independent time, bringing their folder to the carpet with just one piece on the outside of their folder. This makes share time more efficient, so kids aren't searching for the piece of writing that they will talk about.

⑤ During Work Time

Create a quiet space for partners to meet. A designated partner space allows you to monitor how many partnerships are meeting and for how long they are meeting. Perhaps only one partnership can use this space at a time. A sand timer could denote how long partnership meetings last before writers return to their individual writing work.

Convey a "be respectful when writers are having a conference" message, and have the words "Wait, listen in" on the back side of your clipboard, ready to display as a reminder.

④ Signals that Gather Students' Attention during Work Time

"Writers can you stop, writers can you look, writers can you listen?"

or

Teacher: One, two, three, eyes on me!

Kids: One, two, eyes on you!

or

Teacher (to the tune of "Frère Jacques"):
Can you find me? Can you find me?
Here I am! Here I am!

① Before the Minilesson

Lost and Found

Once partnerships are established, a child whose partner is absent can go to a designated spot near the meeting area to connect with another child whose partner is also missing.

The "Writers Prepare!" chart can be found in the online resources.

② During the Minilesson

Children are ideally gathered together in a meeting space in a way that allows them to see and hear the teacher while also being able to easily interact with one or more writers. It can be helpful to create sections within the space such as a center aisle that will allow for the teacher to interact with the children during a turn-and-talk.

③ Releasing from Minilesson

Gradual Release

Prompt students who are ready to go and begin work, "When you have an idea for the cover you will draw, off you go!" Kids who remain need more support.

No Question Zone

During this portion of the workshop—usually the first two or three minutes—let kids know you won't entertain any questions. This supports kids in solving their own problems and answering their own questions.

Sweep and Compliment

After the minilesson, sweep across your classroom, complimenting writers. Positive narration will settle writers and make your presence felt around the room.

This description of each part of the writing workshop can be found in the online resources.

Setting Up Your Writing Workshop 4

Setting Up Your Writing Workshop

Teaching writing does not require elaborate materials or special classroom arrangements. There are, however, a few room arrangements that especially support the teaching of writing. If I took you on a tour of any one of the thousands of schools where writing workshops flourish, you'd begin to notice the distinctive room arrangements even before we stepped into particular classrooms. Even as we walked along the corridor, peeking into classrooms, you would see that in most of these classrooms, there are spaces for students to gather, spaces for them to write, and spaces for writing tools and resources to be stored.

Use of the Classroom Space

The Meeting Area: A Space for Gathering

In most workshop classrooms, one corner has been filled with a large carpet framed on several sides with bookcases, creating a library area that doubles as a meeting space. These carpets (and the communities that are created as classes gather on them) are important. In fact, after being promoted to the position of a New York City superintendent, a longtime TCRWP principal greeted me by saying, "Lucy, you'll be glad to know we put carpets into over one thousand classrooms already."

Usually, there's a low chair for you at the head of the meeting area, flanked by an easel with chart paper and a document camera or a Smart Board within easy reach as you sit in that chair. If outlets make it hard for your tech equipment to be within reach and low, get an extension cord! You'll use this technology to share your evolving demonstration writing and examples of kids' writing, and, of course, to enlarge mentor texts.

Your teaching each day will be encapsulated in a teaching point that gets added to the anchor chart for that unit, which will be prominently displayed. Many teachers laminate the sticky notes that accompany the unit so they can easily recycle them year after year. We do not advise laminating the entire anchor chart, because doing so ruins the gradual reveal as you recap your minilesson by adding a new teaching point to the chart.

When children gather for minilessons or share sessions, you'll probably give them assigned seats. Organize your seating chart so partners sit beside each other in long rows that begin as close to your seat as possible. This allows you to listen in easily as kids in the first two rows talk. Some teachers prefer a middle aisle so they can have easier access to listening in on the conversations that occur in the back two rows. Many teachers assign one child in each partnership to be Partner 1, the other, Partner 2, and often designate which partner talks first or is the talker during brief partner interactions. This prevents the more dominant partner from always usurping most of the talk time.

Work Areas: Spaces for Writing, Small Groups, and Conferring

Although the corner meeting area is a trademark of classrooms that are organized to support workshop instruction, the far more important spaces are those in which your kids sustain their work as writers. The goal during work time is for kids to work with high levels of engagement and with enough independence that you are free to lead small groups and conferences.

Usually children work at tables or at desks that have been clustered together to form table-like seating arrangements, sitting alongside their writing partner. If kids keep their stuff in cubbies, not desks, these writing spots may not be their permanent seats. Most classrooms also have a few work spots that are referred to as "private offices" and that allow children to work away from congestion.

You may worry about dispersing seating areas around the room. Will all children have a view of the texts you display using a document camera or smart board? This is not a problem, because mostly you show documents when youngsters are gathered for minilessons or share sessions. The teaching you tend to do mid-workshop won't usually require children's eyes to be on a particular text. Also, if some children's work spots don't provide the perfect visual

access, you can invite those children to shift their seating spots when necessary.

Encouraging kids to get out of their seats when they need to do so is important in general. Your students will need visual access to charts, to the alphabetically organized word wall, and to additional writing paper, as well as tools such as scissors and tape.

As children work, I encourage you to move among them rather than call them up to your table or desk. It's helpful for you to be in the midst of your writers, because this allows you to watch and learn from the work they are doing. But it is also marvelous for the kids to be able to eavesdrop on your conferences and small groups. I encourage you to say to kids, "If you need me, don't stay in your seat with your hand raised. Instead, come to where I am and listen in until I can help you." If you have a line of kids needing you, just circle them around you as you teach so they all have front row seats, and after you complete a conference or a small group, you can say, "How does that pertain to your writing?" Usually it will be surprisingly relevant.

Tips for Making Charts that Support Instruction and Encourage Independence

There are many tips you can draw on to make charts that support instruction or encourage independence:

- Make sure the heading names a big skill or goal so that children know the purpose of the chart.
- Use visuals (photos, icons, exemplars) to allow children to get a lot of information at a glance.
- Construct the charts in the presence of children. For example, have children add their names (on sticky notes) next to strategies tried, or add student examples to strategies.

- Reread the charts with your whole class often.
- Make small copies of charts and give selected charts to children to carry with them.
- Send charts home to keep caregivers abreast of your instruction.

Provisioning Your Writing Workshop

Although writing workshops do not require fancy materials—you don't need much more than pens and paper, at a minimum—the flip side is that materials can make an exponential difference to your teaching. If you have paper of all sorts in booklets tailored for the genre in which kids are writing, and if you provide kids with markers and sticky notes, folders and envelopes, staplers, and brads and scissors, those tools can coax children to love writing. The units will show you how these tools can be imbued with power.

For example, it makes the world of difference to be able to give children purple markers when you want them to revise. "Use these, the color of royalty," you can say, to celebrate children's revisions. When you want children to learn to reread their writing from the perspective of a stranger, they'll be far more likely to do that if you give them big sticky notes on which to record what they think that readers will be wondering. And children are much more apt to write persuasive letters to authors if they've got stamp pads to turn their paper into stationary, complete with thumbprint caterpillars and spiders.

The basics: kids need paper and folders to hold their writing.

But let's start with the basics. You need paper and a way to save student writing. In the online resources for every unit, we provide examples of the paper that we hope is perfect for that unit. We will always suggest several options so you can adjust the paper for writers needing different levels of support. Use these, making sure that you move kids to more challenging paper as soon as they are ready for it.

Lines and Picture Boxes

For young children, the number of lines on a page matters a lot. The size of the picture box matters too. More lines will either coax kids to write more or shut kids down and make them feel overwhelmed. As the year unfolds, you will often say to individual children, "I think you are ready to graduate to a new kind of paper. This is a huge step, and it means that you'll want to . . ." The point is that the paper needs to march just ahead of what students can do, so that it nudges them to write more, to grow more.

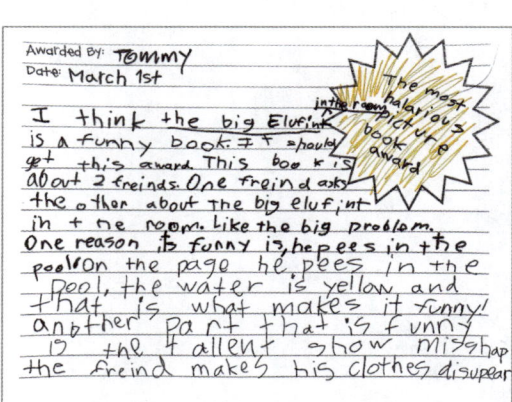

FIG. 4–1 Page structure, including number of lines and space for images, will vary depending on the age and ability of the writer. These are first pages to a How-To book and a review.

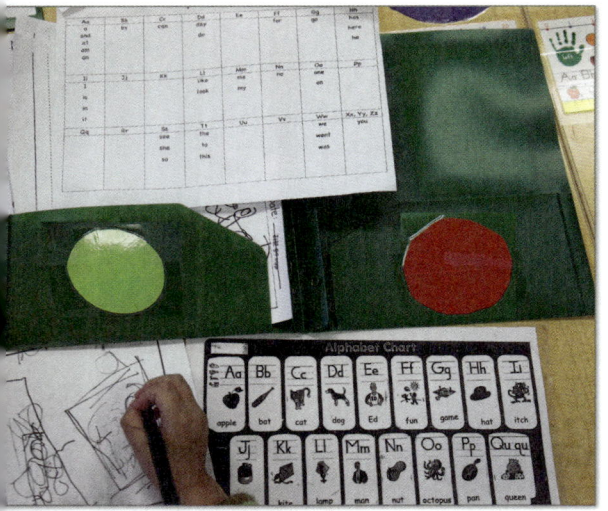

Quantity and Storage of Writing

Not only is paper helpful for conveying expectations for the volume of writing you hope kids produce, it also reminds kids of the structure within which they are writing. For example, imagine how helpful it will be if a child writing a How-To book is given paper with boxes down the left side, with each box accompanied by four or five lines.

In most K–2 writing classrooms, teachers find it helpful to give each child a writing folder and a place for children to store their folders. Children who sit at the blue table, for example, have a blue box for their blue-dotted folders. When writing workshop begins, a table monitor brings the box of folders to each table. Children remove the piece that they are working on and any relevant charts from that folder, usually then returning the folder to the box, leaving their work areas relatively unencumbered.

All of the child's recent work within a unit is kept in the folder. Folders are usually emptied out after a unit, with the finished work either going home or going into cumulative folders. You probably won't send work home until your first parent-teacher conference, when you'll be able to talk about (and by then, to demonstrate) the ways each child's spelling has already developed. If you send writing home without communication about invented spelling, some parents may misunderstand your approach to spelling, thinking you have lax, rather than demanding, expectations, when the opposite is true.

The work is dated each day with that day's date stamp. This makes it very easy for you to look through a child's folder and re-create what the child did in the writing workshop on Monday, Tuesday, Wednesday, and so on. Most teachers put a green dot (for "Go") on the left side of the folder as a way to signal that this is a place for current work, and a red dot on the right signaling that this work has stopped.

Why not use notebooks and journals for K–2 writers?

We urge you *not* to channel your K–2 children to write in bound or spiral notebooks. For young children, the writing workshop is a time to make stuff, and that stuff has physical dimensions that matter. It's true that, starting in fourth grade, we encourage children to keep a writer's notebook. But the writer's notebooks that children keep in upper-grade classrooms are part of an entire system of sustained commitment to a text across days, with kids shifting from notebooks to folders.

Children find it is vastly more compelling to produce all the kinds of writing they see in the world. Constructing the physical artifact of a book, a letter, a recipe, a poem, a speech is a big deal. The cover, the sequence of pages, the final page, the back cover—all of that is a big deal. Usually, when journals are brought into K–2 classrooms, they become containers for writing that has no genre and no audience (other than perhaps the teacher) and that is never revised, edited, or published.

Kids need writing utensils and revision tools.

Some supplies need to be available always, starting with pens or markers. In most classrooms, these tools are communally owned and kept in caddies, one for each table, with table monitors assigned to bring those caddies to the tables. Teachers often ask parents to contribute to the community supply. Or, because costs decrease with quantity, you might ask parents to chip in a few dollars toward a class caddy for markers, pens, and pencils. Many supplies that are ordered at the start of the year will be withheld until they are needed.

We recommend that kindergartners start the year with sturdy marker pens and first-graders with thinner marker pens. Before too long, you'll channel them to nonmarker pens or the slightly less ideal option of pencils. Many teachers keep a can of sharpened pencils in each toolbox and ask children to avoid sharpening pencils during the writing workshop. Instead, the entire set of pencils is sharpened as part of morning jobs. If a child breaks a pencil point, the child puts the broken pencil in the "to be sharpened" can. Most teachers suggest that if children write with pencils, it is best if they do not use erasers. After all, any teacher will want to see and admire children's drafts and revisions!

You will want to have children alter their writing tools as the year progresses. At some point, you might announce that because writers have grown so much, now, instead of coloring, they will do the professional work of sketching—and they'll do this so they can focus more on writing and double their expected volume. In this way, you make the transition from markers to pens into a graduation of sorts.

As soon as you have taught your students to revise (or reminded them they know how to do this), make sure the toolboxes contain scissors and tape. When writers have learned to date their work, you'll want to include a date stamp. All of these things— the scissors and tape, the date stamp, the different dots on kids' writing folders—are revealed to kids with some fanfare as the Units of Study unfold. It isn't helpful for you to do these preparations before the year begins.

Kids need mentor texts and other examples of the sort of things they are making.

An immersion in a variety of great literature is enormously important. As Annie Proulx says, "You should write because you love the shape of stories and sentences and the creation of different words on a page. Writing comes from reading, and reading is the finest teacher of how to write." How important it is to provide children with the richest possible library, including books filled with characters who offer young readers both windows and mirrors. It's also important to give them lots of time to read. Kids absolutely need to marinate themselves in texts that are like those they hope to write.

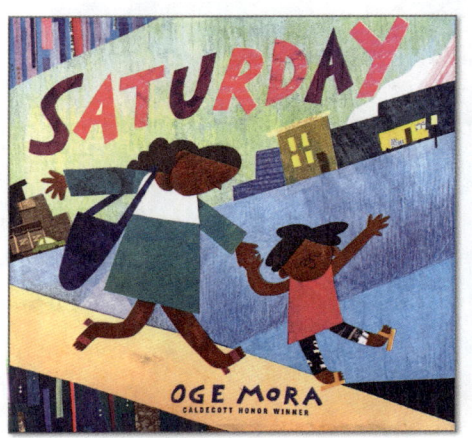

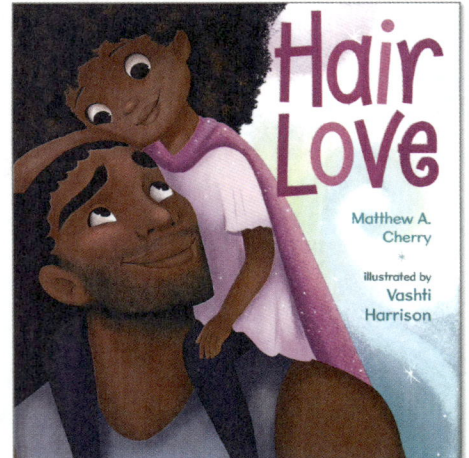

Rereading books will inspire your own writing.

You'll see that, for every unit, we've chosen just a small stack of mentor texts, which students return to over and over. When Hemingway was asked, "How do I learn to write?" he answered, "Read *Anna Karenina*, read *Anna Karenina*, read *Anna Karenina*." That's potent advice. Writers especially learn to write by *re*reading. A writer finds a text that he or she loves, one that matches the sort of thing that writer is trying to make. The writer rereads that text over and over, studying the craft moves the author has made and the effect those moves have on readers. Then the writer thinks, "Maybe I could try that!" and after yet more study, the writer turns to his own draft, thinking, "Where could I try that same work?"

To emulate an author, to learn craft moves from an author, it is incredibly important for writers to revisit a few deeply familiar and well-loved texts over and over. They should note places where the text gets through to them and then turn the text inside out to ask, "What did the writer do here that I could try?"

> *"Writing comes from reading, and reading is the finest teacher of how to write." —Annie Proulx*

We hope you teach kids that when they reread a mentor text, they can apply different lenses to each reread, paying attention one time to the author's word choices, another time to the text's structure. Perhaps, for example, you want kids to learn that sometimes the ending of a text circles back to the text's beginning. In instances such as this, you might say, "Will you look at this mentor text and notice the way the author....?"

Finding the Right Level of Mentor Text

As Vygotsky's (1978) research reminds us, mentor texts that are within a learner's zone of proximal development are especially helpful. Therefore, there will be many instances when you either use a child's writing or your own constructed writing as a mentor text. For example, when teaching a kindergarten child to label items in her drawing—writing an *S* beside the sun, a *B* beside the bike—it's useless to look for published mentor texts to illustrate this work.

Mentor texts are also not ideal for showing children the steps writers take to construct one kind of text or another. You'll want, therefore, to engage in public writing of demonstration texts, weaving such a text through most bends in most units. Plan to return to that draft often to show students whatever new writing process step skill you are teaching. Most units include a demonstration text that you can adopt as your own if you like, tweaking it to make it more reflective of you while maintaining the craft of the text. You can also echo-write your own text, illustrating the same strategies as does the mentor text that is already woven into the unit.

Writers don't need much: paper, a pen, a place to store their writing, a few wonderful published texts, and time. Because writers don't need much, it is entirely possible for a school system to provide writing workshops with all that is needed, and doing so is enormously important. I've watched writing workshops take hold within a year or two in every classroom up and down the corridors of a school. When I tried to discern the conditions that made it likely that teachers and children embrace the writing workshop, I discovered that provisioning workshops with the necessary materials, and teachers with the units, actually makes a world of difference. Throughout the history of the human race, tools have made us smarter. The stylus, the computer—these tools of the hand become habits of the mind, re-creating what it means to live and learn together.

Clear and Ambitious Expectations for All

A group of principals recently joined me in visiting the classroom of a new first-year teacher. The writing workshop was about to begin. "Writers," Alexi said, "let's gather." As if on cue, Alexi's twenty-eight children gathered on the carpet, each sitting on top of a decorated writing folder, shoulder to shoulder with a long-term writing partner. Alexi began leading a ten-minute minilesson in which she named a strategy that writers often use. She then demonstrated that strategy, gave her children a few minutes of guided practice with the strategy, and invited them to add that strategy to their repertoire. Soon, the children had dispersed to their writing spots, each hard at work on his or her own ongoing writing project. None of them required Alexi to come to over and provide a personalized jump start.

How was this possible for a brand-new teacher? As we reflected on this question, the principals and I realized that although Alexi was new to the profession, *her methods* weren't new. Her methods have gone through hundreds of drafts and have been shaped by the legacy of scores of experienced teachers. Then too, efficient management comes from children, as well as teachers, having clear and ambitious expectations. Clearly, Alexi's children enter her classroom already knowing what their jobs are during minilessons and work time. All of this meant that even as a first-year teacher, Alexi was able to nurture her little crew of writers into becoming a *community*, a group of individuals with a shared set of norms, expectations, and purposes. Her year was well on the way!

Ideas for How to Set Up Your Classroom

The Minilesson

The Minilesson

J ust as the art instructor pulls students together to learn a new glaze or the football coach huddles his team to go over a new play—you will pull children together for minilessons that open each day's writing workshop.

Minilessons are meant as intervals for explicit, brief instruction in skills and strategies that then become part of a writer's ongoing repertoire, to be drawn upon as needed. That is, every day in a writing workshop, you gather the learners and say, "I've been thinking about the work you are doing, and I want to give you just one tip, one technique that I think will help with challenges some of you are encountering, or will soon." Then you demonstrate the new technique and help children get a bit of assisted practice trying it in miniature ways, all within a ten-minute minilesson. After this, you send learners off to continue their important work, reminding them that they can draw on the strategy they learned that day, as well as those they've learned on previous days.

I've often said that the most important words of any workshop are the words that come at the end, when you say, "Off you go." In any workshop, it is important that the kids know how to do just that. They need to know that after the minilesson is over, they can resume the important work they were doing the day before, drawing on all they have learned all year long and, especially, over the recent weeks. Then, at the end of each day's workshop, you'll gather your writers once more, bringing that day's work to a close with a brief time to share. The share often harkens back to the teaching of the minilesson, and brings a sense of closure to the workshop, just as the minilesson provides a sense of welcome.

Learning to Lead Effective Minilessons

When school leaders ask us, "How do I help teachers get started with Units of Study?" we usually suggest they start by supporting people to lead effective minilessons. In professional development, teachers often read over a minilesson, imagining how they might teach it, and then watch a video of a TCRWP staff developer leading that same minilesson. After a follow-up discussion to talk about ways the staff developer's teaching was different than their own, they return to the same video of an effective minilesson, this time watching with much more specificity. What are time-saving moves the staff developer makes? How does the staff developer keep kids engaged? When does—and when doesn't—the staff developer look at the unit of study book or otherwise read something? How is—and isn't—technology used?

Key Features of The Minilesson

- To convene a minilesson, many teachers have a signal they use repeatedly. Perhaps this is some music that signals, "Let's transition." Perhaps a child is sent from table to table, like a young Paul Revere, saying "Writing time." Other teachers sing out a chorus such as the one that goes, "Stop, look, and listen," whereupon children freeze, look at the teacher, and then sing back in a lovely echo, "Oh, yeah." In the quietness after this exchange, these teachers talk to the writers—quietly, not in a playground voice—saying, "Will you bring your writing folder and come join me in the meeting area?"

- Many teachers find it efficient to ask children to always bring their writing folders (which generally contain a marker, pencil, or pen slid into the pocket) to every minilesson. If children sit on their folders, the materials will stay out of the way of fiddling fingers, yet be accessible when needed.

- The aura of a minilesson is more like a whole-class read-aloud (or a huddle at the start of a football game) than a lecture. Minilessons feel like intimate and urgent gatherings. "Listen up!" the teacher says, leaning forward in the chair, looking kids in the eyes. Minilessons are about as far from PowerPoint lectures as you can get.

- Visuals, gestures, dramatization, and changes in intonation all help keep kids engaged.

- Minilessons also include silent moments for kids to think or point or "write-in-the-air," and above all, frequent "turn-and-talk intervals." Kids learn to switch quickly from listening to you, to talking with a partner, then back to listening to you.

- When kids are talking to partners, you usually listen—and sometimes you take a second to orient yourself for the next bit of teaching. After a minute, you sometimes say to the group, "I heard you say. . . " in which case you might recap what you heard.

- Because minilessons are so short, they aren't occasions for reading or writing whole texts. Instead, you are apt to thread a text through many minilessons, so that on any one day, you zoom in only on the part of the text that you are spotlighting.

- You rarely write more than a sentence or two in a minilesson. If you want to produce more than two or three lines of writing, just touch the page and say the words, then turn that into enlarged writing on chart paper another time.

The Architecture of Minilessons

You may notice that every minilesson follows the same predictable architecture. When you are preparing to teach a minilesson, you'll find that your preparation is vastly more efficient if you keep that architecture in mind. While the content of minilessons changes from day to day, the architecture of minilessons remains largely the same, and it remains consistent whether you are teaching reading or writing. Minilessons are only ten minutes long at most, yet within those fleeting minutes are four component parts:

- Connection
- Teaching
- Active Engagement
- Link

Connection

Minilessons start with an effort to both connect with kids and connect today's teaching with the ongoing work that children have been doing. You essentially say, "Listen up," and then you say, "Yesterday we . . ." or "Last year you . . ." or "Last night I looked over your writing and realized . . ." In the first part of your connection, you aim to draw kids in and to help them anticipate how your teaching today will fit into the larger context of what they've been learning. Then, as part of the connection, you state the teaching point. I describe this later.

Use Drama and Sharing to Engage Writers

To engage children, you might pretend your cell phone is buzzing. Bringing the phone to your ear, you pretend to learn that there's a box outside your classroom door. You return with a box labeled "Teacher inside." You and the kids open the box with great drama

and find not a human teacher, but a mentor text. Then again, you might start your minilesson by saying, "Last night I couldn't sleep. I kept thinking about what I could teach you today that would really really help. Then an idea came to me. I jumped out of bed and wrote it on a sticky note so I wouldn't forget. Here's my sticky note."

Orient Kids to Today's Work

To orient kids, you'll often recap what they have already been learning. For example, if you intend to teach a new way to revise, you might start the minilesson by asking the kids to turn to their partner and list three ways they already know to revise. Alternatively, perhaps you and the class chorally read the anchor chart that lists a few ways to revise, with kids signaling yes or no (in some way) for whether they've done that kind of revision. Then again, you could just ask kids to tell a partner ways they revise. Listening in, you could scrawl what you heard (or wished you were hearing) in a list and then pause the conversations to say, "I heard many of you saying these things . . . ," reading aloud the list.

Notice that you are not beginning your minilesson with a barrage of questions. "Class, what did we talk about yesterday? And what did we say about . . . ?" Minilessons are a time for you to talk to the kids, as directly and clearly as you can. After drawing kids into the minilesson and orienting them to today's work, you shift and say the teaching point for the day. This teaching point is the crux of what you will teach. You are apt to repeat it several times in your minilesson and to record it on a sticky note that becomes part of the anchor chart that memorializes today's teaching.

Name the Teaching Point

To signal to your kids that this is the teaching point of the lesson, start your teaching point with a phrase such as "Today I want to teach you . . ." Then put the crux of today's minilesson into words, making sure you are teaching kids something that will help their writing not only today, but often. Teaching points—and indeed, minilessons—are how-to texts. That is, you often will include the goal (worded in such a way that the teaching point is transferable) and the step-by-step procedure. Teaching points name a skill or strategy that writers can use often. Your wording is more apt to be, "I want to teach you that when writers want to come up with a topic, they often think back to . . ." instead of "Today you will . . . ." The teaching point is not an assigned task. The difference is not just a matter of words. It's a difference of intent. In a minilesson, you teach writers something they can do repeatedly, perhaps today and, certainly, for the rest of their lives.

Examples of Teaching Points

- "Today I want to teach you that when you want to bring your writing to life, you can add in the exact words a person said. You can write those in a speech bubble, or you can put them right into your story."

- "Today I want to teach you that to write how-to steps that a reader can easily follow, writers picture themselves doing it—almost like they're watching video in slow motion. And they pause often to say, 'What exact words describe what I just did?'"

- "Today I want to teach you that when writers have an opinion, they give *a couple of reasons*, not just one, to support that reason. For each reason, they add some details about that reason. They use phrases like *for example* or *I think that because* to bring in some details."

Teaching

Teaching within a minilesson is challenging, because you have just a very few minutes to teach something that they can use for the rest of their lives.

Your teaching focuses on pointers.

To keep your minilesson brief, it helps to remember that in any one minilesson, you will not support the entire writing process. You zoom in on one specific aspect of it. For example, you won't, in one day, show writers how to choose an issue that matters to them, decide on an audience for their efforts, figure out what they're arguing for, and also

generate reasons to support that opinion. If the day's minilesson is designed to encourage writers to provide reasons to support their opinion, then your focus is only on generating reasons to support an opinion, and the writing you do in the minilesson will add reasons to an *already existing* persuasive letter.

This means that you usually work on one piece of writing across a sequence of minilessons. The kids will come to know your draft well, so on any given day, your teaching can spotlight just a part of it. For example, you might teach kids that when writing information books, it helps to think about the questions that readers will probably ask. To illustrate that, you can rally kids to join you in rereading your All-About book, anticipating readers' questions, and noting places for revision. You wouldn't actually do that revision while in the meeting area.

Connect writing to lived experience.

Another way to make the teaching brief and yet potent is to teach about qualities of writing by talking about something the kids have seen or experienced, that at first has very little to do with writing. So if you wanted to teach kids that it helps to write not just with any ol' details, but with *surprising* details, you could turn to the beach as your example, saying, "I could write that the beach had white sand, but beaches tend to have white sand. That isn't really a surprising detail. It'd be more powerful to write, 'Long ribbons of seaweed were scattered over the beach.'" If you want to teach about the way the setting can create a mood, you can show a photo of a stormy day and ask kids to name the mood the photo creates. They can contrast that with the mood created by a photo of a sunny day and then hear that writers create setting to influence the changing mood in a story.

Four Methods for Teaching

It can help to realize that within the three-minute-long teaching portion of a minilesson, you can use any one of four methods of teaching.

Demonstration (Including Step-by-Step Directions)

Imagine, for a moment, that you were teaching someone to put on their shoes. You'd probably first remove your shoes, then you'd say something like, "Watch me. Notice what I do and then you can try it." Then you'd proceed slowly, in a step-by-step way, to put on one of your shoes, chronicling the steps as you did them, tucking in little pointers. ("Sometimes you need to wiggle your foot from right to left a bit to get it actually into the shoe.") Once the shoe was securely on, you might do a quick recap before saying, "Your turn. Try putting your own shoe on now." The vast majority of minilessons employ this method.

Guided Practice

There are other options for shoe-tying instruction—and for your writing workshop. You could lead the learner through a step-by-step process while keeping your own shoes securely on your feet. "Start by pointing your toe," you could say. Then after the learner did that, you could press on: "That's it. Now stick that pointed toe right into the shoe, all the way to the far end of it." That instruction (if continued) is what I refer to as guided practice.

Explain-and-Give-an-Example

Another method you could use to teach this lesson is one that I refer to as explain-and-give-an-example. This tends to be less memorable for kids. It essentially involves giving a little lecture, complete with illustrations. You could go so far as to create a PowerPoint presentation with an illustrated chart showing the four stages of foot insertion.

Inquiry

Finally, you could teach by simply saying, "How do you think I got this shoe on my foot?" And that would be inquiry. This method is most common when you want to engage youngsters in studying an example of good work. Pulling your students together, you say, "How do you think this author wrote such an effective ending to her speech?" Then you and the students generate a list of things the author has done that they could also try.

Active Engagement

After you teach something in your minilesson, you'll give children the opportunity to try what you've taught for just a minute or two while sitting in the meeting area, supported by the other kids and you.

Writing-in-the-Air

In the example described earlier, after teaching kids to add surprising details and using the beach as an example, you might suggest kids turn to partners and apply what they've learned about writing with details to a piece they might write. To make this activity proceed quickly, you might ask everyone to try writing with details while telling about a "practice topic" you assign—a topic they'll use only in the minilesson. For example, you might suggest writers practice writing with details as they write about one writer's hand. You'll save time by asking them to "write-in-the-air," which means dictating what they would write if time allowed. Once the partners get started doing that, you could coach in a voiceover, "My hand has five fingers, but hands tend to have five fingers. Look more closely. Really see your hand and reach for exact, true, and surprising details."

Rereading Writer's Work

Then again, you might help writers write with details by saying, "Will Partner 1 take out your writing? Will you and Partner 2 reread it, seeing if together, you can find a place where you could add a surprising detail into that writing?" Then, as kids work, you listen in, saying aloud a few especially strong examples.

Guiding Partner Work During Minilessons

It'll pay off for you to explicitly teach youngsters to be effective partners. You might spotlight partnerships that are especially good at helping each other. You might role-play being an ineffective partner, contrasting it with you being a helpful partner. "Watch my partner and me," you might say, roping in a student teacher so that you can reenact some of the horseplay you have seen kids doing with *their* partners. "Does this look like we're making smart use of our partner time?" Children will chorus, "Noooo." Then, for contrast, you can say, "*Now* watch my partner and me," and this time look your partner in the eyes, nod responsively as she talks, and so forth. You might make little asides as you do this, muttering, "Oh, what a great question! I love that question she asked!" or "Don't you love how she listens? I feel like she's really interested."

Link

Pulitzer prize–winning writer Donald Murray once told me that the single most important sentence in a paragraph is the last one. "This sentence needs to propel readers onward to the next paragraph," he said. "It needs to be not a closing, but a launch." Remember this advice when you reach the final part of your minilessons. These last few sentences need to encapsulate the content of the minilesson in such a way that kids get their mental arms around that content and carry it with them as they head off from your teacher-led work into the whole of their writing lives.

Making a Difference Beyond Today's Lesson

The challenge when teaching is always to make a real difference—a challenge that is not for the faint of heart. It's a tall order. It helps to remind children that any one day's particular teaching point is part of a larger repertoire of strategies that they will be drawing upon. This often means that in the link, you will reference an anchor chart (presumably the same one that was mentioned in the connection). When doing this, you'll want to remind children that the goal is not just to do the work of today's minilesson, but also to draw on what is now an even larger repertoire of strategies. You'll also want to remind them that, throughout their lives, writers always call upon their growing repertoire of strategies. You'll start the link by saying something such as, "Whenever you are in this writing situation and you want to . . . , you can draw on this technique. . . . "

> *The challenge when teaching is always to make a real difference—a challenge that is not for the faint of heart.*

The link, of course, also needs to channel students to actually accomplish something concrete today, so this will also be a time for brass tacks: what kind of paper, where that paper is accessible, what one might do first and next, and what is expected by when.

Sending Children Off to Work with Purpose

Then, there is the actual send-off. Early in the year, especially, you might disperse children in clusters. While one cluster goes off to work, you might say to those who are still sitting on the carpet, "Let's watch and see if those writers *zoom* to their writing spots and get started right away!" Then, as the remaining class joins you in watching the children who are getting started on their work, you might celebrate the writers who are being especially industrious, saying, for example, "Oh, look! Jon has his paper out and his folder put neatly away! He's rereading what he wrote yesterday! How industrious!" Of course, the other dispersing youngsters will hear you discussing the cluster and they'll respond in all the expected ways.

Sometimes you will disperse children by saying, "If you are going to be doing [one kind of work] today, get going." Then you will say, "If you are going to be doing [another kind of writing work] today, get going." Finally you may say, "If you are not sure what to do today and need some help, stay here and I'll work with you"—and soon you're leading a small group of children who've identified themselves as needing more direction.

Helping Writers Be as Engaged as Possible during Minilessons, without Sacrificing Brevity

Teach children how minilessons tend to go, so they know when it will be their turn to listen, to talk, and to practice that day's strategy or tip.

Before the connection: Say, "Today and every day in the minilesson, when I say, 'Writers, let's gather,' you'll get your writing folder and hurry here. You'll sit on your folders and you'll sit on your rug spot with your writing partner beside you. Then I'll talk to you for a few minutes. When I talk to you, you're going to really turn your brains on to high [you'll act this out] and *listen*, because I'm going to show you a strategy you'll want to use in your writing. You'll do a lot of listening during that first part of the minilesson, and not a lot of talking.

"Then, after I show you something I hope will be helpful to you, you'll have time to try the strategy yourself, right here on the rug. Usually you'll turn to your partner and do some work together. Then, after the minilesson, you'll go off to your writing spots, and you'll carry the new strategy with you and use it as you write your own pieces on topics you choose."

During teaching: As you begin, say, "Hmm, . . . how shall I . . . ?" or "Join me as I . . ." Then, after leaving a little space for all learners to consider how they'd do this work, you push ahead and start doing whatever it is you want to teach. Because you invited your students to consider how they'd do this and left a little space for them to imagine how they'd start doing it, they can be comparing what they were about to do with whatever you do. Then, of course, during **active engagement**, you'll say, "Your turn," and set up children to either write-in-the-air or turn and talk with a partner.

Then again, you will sometimes say to youngsters, "Right now, decide what you need to do today while you sit here on the rug. Then get started. When I see that you are well launched, I'll send you off to your writing spot." That way, you can support the transition to writing, disperse children one at a time once they clearly have some momentum, and quickly spot and support children needing help.

Share

In addition to the minilesson, the other part of the workshop designated for whole-class teaching is the share. The minilesson and the share bookend each day's workshop.

Sharing at Tables or in the Meeting Area

The shares serve as reminders that even though writers are working independently on their own pieces, the class is working together toward a shared mission and with a shared vision. Sometimes, you'll ask students to remain at their seats for the share and to perhaps talk with a partner or their tablemates. More frequently, you'll gather students back in the meeting area. You'll particularly want to gather your class if you are sharing a visual or reading something to the group, or if you want to orchestrate a brief conversation with everyone. Next to the share in each session in the unit books, we've included an icon to indicate whether we recommend gathering the children in the meeting area 🟡, or asking them to share from their table spots 🔶.

Transitioning to the Share

When it is almost time for the class to stop work for the share session, a child might circle the room, letting children know it is time to finish up. Alternatively, you could intervene to announce, "Three more minutes." In any case, writers will need a bit of time to finish what they are writing. Then you'll decide whether, for this share, you will bring children to the meeting area or work with them while they are in their writing spots.

You will want to draw upon a handful of ways that share time generally goes in your classroom and to induct children into those traditions right from the start. Share sessions fairly often involve partnership conversations. The sessions usually highlight the work of one student that the rest of the class might use as a model and celebrate the strong writing work students have done that day. The teacher has a teaching point to make in the share, and she makes it while also helping children reflect on how one aspect of their work went.

Format Options for the Share

You'll probably begin the share by talking with children for a minute or two. You may plan to share one child's work, either by reading the child's work aloud or by asking the child to do so. Then, typically, there is usually time for children to talk with their partners.

Children may alternatively hear the story of a child who tried a strategy you recommended in that day's minilesson. "Nicole reread and, lo and behold, she too found that she had left something out, and look at what she did! Nicole used a caret to fix her story!" Usually you'll not only share but extend students' work. "Nicole found, however, that it was important not only to add information, but also to subtract information. Notice how she crossed out these parts. They didn't go with her topic. You might think about whether you could subtract as well as add to make your writing better."

Finding Share Rituals that Work for Your Class

You won't always follow the shares that are written into the units. You'll also invent your own. To do so, you'll probably select a format that works well for you and use it often. Some teachers like to use partnership shares when children are sharing work and use table shares when children are talking over their ways of solving a particular writing problem. That is, if your goal in the share is to encourage children to talk about how they might end their stories, then you might suggest they have a table conversation to brainstorm ideas. Some teachers use those table conversations as a prelude to a community meeting, which probably involves convening in the meeting area.

Alternatively, you may find that in your classroom, the ritual I describe as a symphony share works well. In this ritual, you ask children to search for an instance when they did something well. For example, you may have taught children that when writing opinion pieces, they need to state their opinion and provide a reason for that opinion. You may have asked children to find a place in their text where they give a reason for their opinion. "When I tip my baton to you, would you read out one instance when you gave a reason for your opinion?" you might say, and then function like the conductor in a symphony, with one child after another reading a contribution. You could do these symphony shares often.

Then again, you may often use a museum share, suggesting youngsters lay their work out so others can admire it, then send children circulating through the room, leaving sticky notes full of compliments. You and your colleagues will invent yet other go-to ways to wind up your workshops.

Conferring

*The Heart of Your Teaching
in a Writing Workshop*

6

Conferring

The Heart of Your Teaching in a Writing Workshop

The writing process approach to teaching writing was once called "the conferring approach to teaching writing," a testimony to the centrality of the writing conference in any writing workshop classroom. When learning to teach writing, learning to confer well will have enormous payoffs because your conferences inform every aspect of your writing instruction. They help you generate strong, responsive teaching every day, and they inform your small groups, mid-workshop teaching points, and minilessons.

The Meaning of Conferring

Here's the thing: even if you are utterly new to the teaching of writing, you know a lot about conferring. The person who cuts your hair confers with you, as does your literacy coach, your principal, your fitness coach, your doctor. Recall any person who has given you advice, and ask yourself, "What did that person do that worked for me? What didn't work?" The answers you develop can guide your conferring.

Conferring Can Help or Hurt

To be more specific, recall the times when someone coached you in ways that moved you palpably forward; what did that person do and how can you do something similar when you work with young writers? Think also about times when someone came into your life and offered you some critique and tips in ways that still hurt you today. What made those interactions so hard for you, and how can you use that to guide your interactions with children? Your conferences with young writers will be vastly more powerful if you draw upon the deep pools of wisdom that you have within yourself about what makes for good one-to-one support.

Above all, remember that when you interact with kids about their writing, you have extraordinary power—either to harm or to help. With that power comes responsibility. Take these interactions seriously. Know that in these brief conversations, you can give children concepts of themselves and knowledge about writing that can make a world of difference. There's a lot of talk about how some teachers have low expectations for kids, but, frankly, some of us have low expectations for ourselves. It's easy to forget that we have enormous power to change a child's life forever, for better or for worse. The smallest word, touch, or gesture can make so much difference.

Conferring Inspires Growth

Think for a moment about the gestures people have made that built you up. Did anyone ever listen as you read your writing aloud? Did that person pull in closer, with eyes welling? Did anyone ever send your writing out to a reader—to your grandfather, your neighbor? Did someone let slip a phrase like, "a writer like you . . ."? Give those same gestures to the young people in your care.

Keep in mind that the cardinal rule of all writing conferences is that the writer needs to leave a wanting to write. The writer's energy for writing should go up, not down. The level of a child's writing, too, should go up. As John Hattie's (2008) research shows, feedback is one of the few things that can actually accelerate a learner's progress. It is amazing to realize that in a conversation that lasts four or five minutes, you can actually send your students' growth curve sky high. This chapter can teach you to confer in ways that matter. Plan to read a bit, then try what you read, then read

> *Above all, remember that when you interact with kids about their writing, you have extraordinary power—either to harm or to help.*

some more. Read it like a cookbook, letting it guide your actions, because you'll learn more from your actions than from my words. Know that when you learn to confer well, this will lift the level of all of your teaching—not only your teaching of writing, but also of every subject. Your methods of teaching will be changed, and that you'll tap into what you learn when you teach reading and math and swimming—even when you teach other teachers.

I remember . . .

one day, a week after I'd first spoken with Don Murray about my writing, I received a letter in the mail from him addressed to "Writer Lucy Calkins." How my heart soared at those words, scrawled on the pale blue envelope. That afternoon, I went to the lumberyard and bought a door, set it on top of two file cabinets, and made myself a desk that was worthy of my new title. Thinking back now, it seems so corny. I was just twenty-three years old! I was in no way the professional writer he was. Murray must surely have been buttering me up. But oh! What a difference his gesture made to that earnest young woman I was at the time.

Years ago, after I worked with fourth-graders at Smith School in Tenafly, New Jersey, I asked one of the youngsters to send me her draft when she finished it. Those were the days when email was a new thing, but Ali's teacher helped and Ali emailed me her story. Her email address was beachgirl@aol.com. I wrote Ali back to thank her for sending the piece of writing, and told her that she should change her email address from "beachgirl" to "powerfulwriter."

Flash-forward to my Tuesday-night graduate class last fall, the first class of the semester. I suggested we begin by having members of this year's new cohort of master's students take turns telling a turning-point story that shed light on why they were now here, starting a program designed to develop the nation's literacy leaders. A young woman introduced herself as Ali Lafferty, and then told the story of how, when she was a fourth-grader, I'd asked her to send her writing to me and when I wrote back, my email said, "You should change your email address from 'beachgirl' to 'powerfulwriter.'" Ali later brought me that email. It was yellow and curled from hanging, for two decades, on her refrigerator door. "That email from you has a lot to do with why I'm in this graduate program," Ali said.

My note to Ali Lafferty all those years ago suggesting she change her email address from "beachgirl" to "powerfulwriter" had the power to change her life course. And the words you use with your students also carry that power. Refer to your children as writers, to their work as drafts. Pull your chair alongside your youngsters, sit eye to eye as if this child is a colleague, and ask those writerly questions that adult writers might ask each other: "What have you been working on as a writer? How do you feel about what you have written so far? Is this one of your best, or is it so-so? What are you thinking you might do to make this even better?" Leave the text in the child's hands while you discuss it, letting your actions convey, "You are in charge." Know that your respectful attentiveness will make the world of difference.

The Architecture of a Conference

Know that there is a predictable architecture to a writing conference, just as there is to a minilesson. Most full conferences include these components:

- **Research** what the child is intending to do and has done.

- **Decide** what to teach and how to teach it, and **compliment** the writer on something you want to support the writer in doing more of.

- **Teach**, often by leading the writer in guided practice, or by naming a teaching point, and showing an example.

- **Link** your conversation to today's work and to the writer's ongoing repertoire of strategies.

Every conference is different and you'll draw on these components with flexibility. In some conferences, you'll minimize the research portion because you approach the conference with goals from previous research. Sometimes a compliment will be the sum total of your entire conference.

Here is an important insight. Although just one part of a conference bears the title *Teach*, the truth is that there is teaching power to every part of a conference.

Research

Think back to that time when a coach or your doctor or your school principal interacted with you in ways that helped. My hunch is that the person started off by listening. We can't help each other unless we first know what the learner is already doing, what hurts, what she is hoping to do and may have already tried. You don't walk into a doctor's office and expect the doctor to diagnose you immediately. Nor do you want your principal to visit your classroom and, without even hearing what you are trying to do, to begin detailing next steps for you. So start a conference by listening. This part of a writing conference is what we call the research phase.

Because it is crucial to begin a conference by understanding what the writer has already been doing, you'll usually begin by watching—even just as you approach

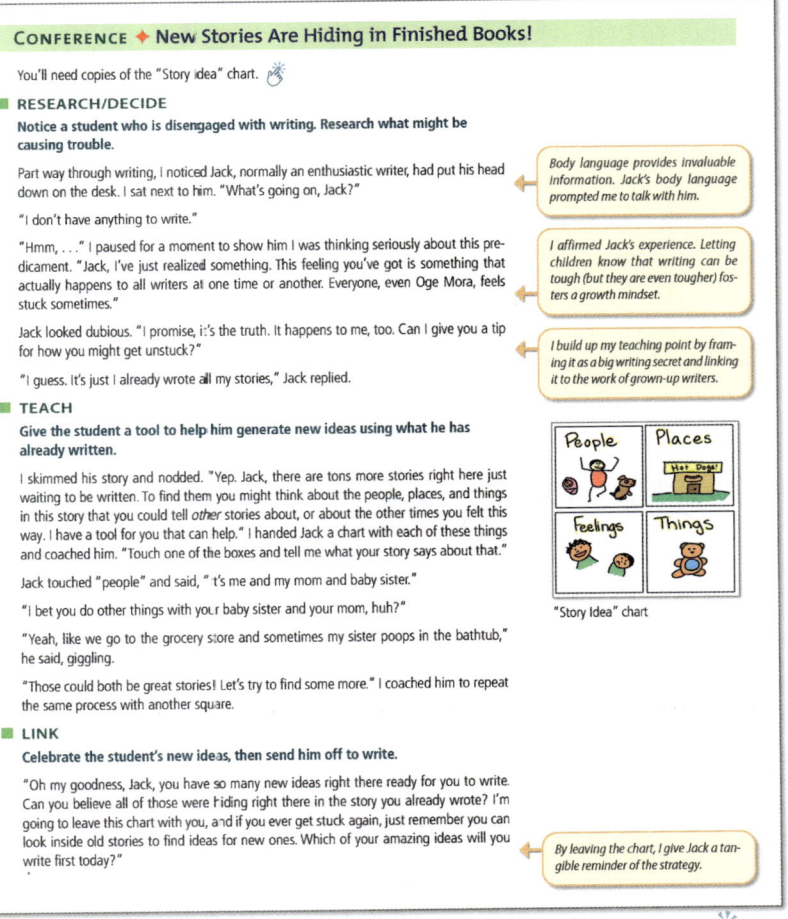

CONFERENCE ◆ New Stories Are Hiding in Finished Books!

You'll need copies of the "Story idea" chart.

■ **RESEARCH/DECIDE**

Notice a student who is disengaged with writing. Research what might be causing trouble.

Part way through writing, I noticed Jack, normally an enthusiastic writer, had put his head down on the desk. I sat next to him. "What's going on, Jack?"

"I don't have anything to write."

"Hmm, . . ." I paused for a moment to show him I was thinking seriously about this predicament. "Jack, I've just realized something. This feeling you've got is something that actually happens to all writers at one time or another. Everyone, even Oge Mora, feels stuck sometimes."

Jack looked dubious. "I promise, it's the truth. It happens to me, too. Can I give you a tip for how you might get unstuck?"

"I guess. It's just I already wrote all my stories," Jack replied.

■ **TEACH**

Give the student a tool to help him generate new ideas using what he has already written.

I skimmed his story and nodded. "Yep. Jack, there are tons more stories right here just waiting to be written. To find them you might think about the people, places, and things in this story that you could tell *other* stories about, or about the other times you felt this way. I have a tool for you that can help." I handed Jack a chart with each of these things and coached him. "Touch one of the boxes and tell me what your story says about that."

Jack touched "people" and said, " t's me and my mom and baby sister."

"I bet you do other things with your baby sister and your mom, huh?"

"Yeah, like we go to the grocery store and sometimes my sister poops in the bathtub," he said, giggling.

"Those could both be great stories! Let's try to find some more." I coached him to repeat the same process with another square.

■ **LINK**

Celebrate the student's new ideas, then send him off to write.

"Oh my goodness, Jack, you have so many new ideas right there ready for you to write. Can you believe all of those were hiding right there in the story you already wrote? I'm going to leave this chart with you, and if you ever get stuck again, just remember you can look inside old stories to find ideas for new ones. Which of your amazing ideas will you write first today?"

Body language provides invaluable information. Jack's body language prompted me to talk with him.

I affirmed Jack's experience. Letting children know that writing can be tough (but they are even tougher) fosters a growth mindset.

I build up my teaching point by framing it as a big writing secret and linking it to the work of grown-up writers.

"Story Idea" chart

By leaving the chart, I give Jack a tangible reminder of the strategy.

This conference, from Grade K, Unit 3, can be found in the online resources.

a writer or as you scan a table, determining which youngsters you want to talk with. Make a point of noticing the writer's all-important engagement in his or her writing.

When you glance at the writer's work, don't look only at the page the writer is working on. Take in a larger swatch of the work. Glance through the folder. Do you find a collection of unfinished booklets there? Do you note more actual writing in the child's recent work? Think about today's work in relation to work from earlier in the year. How much growth are you seeing? Do you note any patterns in the student's writing across time? As you listen and look, your goal is to develop theories about the big work the writer has been doing and may need to do next.

Of course, you will ask the writer questions about her work and plans. Know that the questions you ask writers, in and of themselves, have potent teaching power. You are conveying to writers that the task of writing involves pulling in to writing, pulling back to reread, reflect, question, think, and finally, to revise. Too often kids grow up thinking their job is to write and their teacher's job is to read the draft and guide next steps.

Help children articulate and explain their intentions.

"What are you working on as a writer?" you'll ask. Especially as kids get older (second grade and beyond), you'll teach them that when they respond to this question, they should talk not just about their content ("my dog") or genre and content ("a poem about my dog"), but also about their goals and strategies. ("I'm writing a poem about my dog *and I'm trying to make sure readers can picture my dog, so I'm adding more descriptive words.*") With kindergarten and first-grade children, you may need to ask a sequence of questions to lead the child to teach you these things. That is, if you ask, "What are you working on as a writer?" and the child doesn't seem able to name her intentions, you might decide to look at the child's writing and to name what the child seems to be doing, thereby giving the child words she can eventually use to articulate her intentions. You might say, for example, "I'm noticing that you are revising. It looks like you are adding details to the main part—the most important thing—in your story. Is that right?"

If you ask, "What are you working on as a writer?" or any substitute for that question, and the child launches into the story of what she is writing about, you might hold up your hand like the crossing guard at your school does to stop oncoming traffic and say, "Wait, wait." Then you can steer the child in a different direction. Be sure to explicitly say why you are doing this, explaining, for example, "When I ask, 'What have you been working on as a writer?,' I'm not really wanting to hear what you are writing about, so much as I'm wanting to know what new stuff you are trying to do to get to be an even stronger writer. Like, for example, have you been . . ." You might then point to the anchor chart or fill in some of the answers you anticipate the child producing.

Usually, once a child has told you what he is trying to do, you'll probe to understand what the child means. If the child says, "I'm revising. I'm showing, not telling," you are apt to say, "Can you show me where you did that?" or "Can you tell me more about that?" Of course, you usually have your own understanding of the terms children use (because they give you back the very terms you've taught them). But it is crucial to help a child articulate what *the child* means by "I'm revising" or "I'm fixing up my ending."

Conferences occur in the context of previous conferences, so you can also begin a conference by recalling the last time you and the writer discussed her work, and you can ask, "How has it been, trying to . . . ?" You can then look at progress that resulted from that conversation. For example, you might say, "Last time we talked, you agreed to take the giant step forward of shifting to new paper and trying to write a whole lot more. How has that been for you?" Then you'll follow up by saying, "Can we look at your work since we talked and see if you have actually been able to write more?"

Make sure to pursue more than one line of questioning.

One of the rules of thumb that I especially emphasize is this: once you ask the writer a question about his writing and follow that line of questioning, you'll come to a place where you grasp one thing about the writer and his work. At this juncture, it is tempting to launch into some teaching about that one point. Don't do it! Instead, suspend closure. Don't settle for a single line of inquiry. Be sure to return to a second question, following that one through so that you also understand another aspect of the writer and the work. If you first ask what the child is working on and learn, for example, about his work with the ending of a piece, say, "So one thing you are doing is working on an ending, and to do that you are . . . What are some of the *other* things you plan to do with this piece of writing today?" Of course, that second question could have been entirely different. You could have asked, "How do you feel about this piece? Is it one of your best? Is it just so-so?" You could have asked, "If you were going to fix this piece of writing up so that it is much, much better, what would you do?" As children think about their answers, try to sneak a quick look at the piece of writing so that as you interview the writer, you can also draw on another source of information. One way or another, you will want several sources of information to draw upon as you move to the next phases of a conference.

In the research component of a conference, then, you observe, interview, and read the child's writing (though perhaps only a portion of it) to understand what the child is trying to do as a writer. Because your goal is to bring your students as far as possible along the writing path, and because you know that each conference is a precious opportunity to teach your students only one of the myriad of teaching points available, it is sometimes easy to get stuck doing research fixated on the many things the child does not yet know how to do. Of course, you *do* want to study what the child is not doing to help you decide what new thing to teach. But your conferences will be more successful and meaningful if you take in what the child is working on with your eyes open—particularly to her successes.

Decide/Compliment

A conference, like an iceberg, involves a small amount that is above the surface and far more under the surface. In the moment between the research and the compliment/teach, there is a whole big underground aspect of a writing conference. This is the *decide* part of a conference. In this brief moment, you weigh all of the possible teaching you

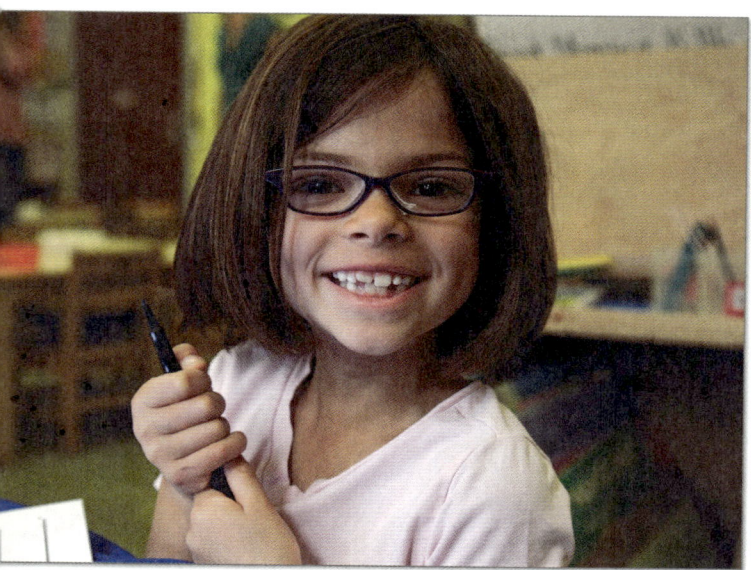

could give, all the directions you could take in the conference, and you choose a course that you think will best power that writer's work. You will also need to decide on a compliment you will give, one that names something the writer is doing well in a way that supports the writer in doing more of that same work.

When deciding what to teach, take the whole of the writer's work into account.

There are steps you can take that will make it more likely that you do this part of the conference well. Start by bringing high expectations for your teaching to the interaction. If you approach a conference intending to glance at the piece of writing, to find one item in the text that doesn't match your internalized checklist for good writing, and then to confer to get the writer to repair that one item—then your conference will feel like an enacted red pen. The writer isn't apt to tell his mom about what you taught him that day, nor to recall it another day.

Start by taking into account more of the student's writing. Look backward at growth over time, scanning to see what the student tends to do often. Think about patterns and habits and idiosyncratic quirks that the youngster seems to bring to many pieces of writing, including the most recent one. Sometimes, you'll even think about the writer's personality, friendships, mindsets, in addition to her writing habits. You then can teach with the specificity of the most recent draft and with the universality and larger scope that comes from addressing the throughline of the writer's life. Here is a compliment that I once gave to a young writer: "Sasha, one thing that really stands out about you is how you include so many tiny details when you write. You put lots of details in your pictures and labels, showing where you were and what the weather was like, and who else was there and how everyone was feeling. All those details help me feel like I'm right there on that playground too! I bet you're the kind of person who pays close attention to everything that's happening around you, no matter where you are. And when you tell and write stories, you make sure to put all the details you remember into your pictures and words. Will you promise to do that forever and ever?" In this example, the compliment gains power because it addresses more than just the piece of writing in hand.

My colleagues and I often lead what we refer to as "conferring clinics" to teach the art of conferring. One portion of a conferring clinic always involves asking teachers to work with each other in ways that allow them to externalize this silent, underground portion of a conference. "Think aloud as you research, and before you compliment," we coach. Then we help the teacher who has assumed the role of conferring coach to prompt the teacher who is conferring by asking questions such as these: "So what are the bigger patterns you see in how this writer tends to work?" "What does the writer tend to do?" "What might be a huge important next step for the writer?" "What are some other options you are considering?" "Which of those might make the biggest difference?"

Offer a compliment that reinforces the kind of work you want the child to replicate, not just in the current piece, but always.

Growing up, my big brother, whom I idolized, had a quote on his bulletin board: "I can live for two months on a good compliment." All these years later, I think of that quote often when I am complimenting a writer. My aim is to give that writer a compliment that will sustain her for two months (or perhaps for twenty years). I know there is not a chance in the world that my conference will matter that much if I don't aim for it to matter in big and lasting ways.

When you're ready to give a compliment, think about the way soda erupts from a shaken soda can and make your compliment feel that way. Look up from the page, pause the writer's talk for just a minute, and let'er rip: "Holy moly, Raphael, what you are saying! Do you have any idea how rare it is for a six-year-old to go back to not just today's writing, but all the writing you did this week, and to think about how you could fix up each piece? Are you sure you are six, not sixty? What you are doing is so grown-up, I can hardly stand it. Would you be willing to become a Professor of Rereading and teach other kids in the class about how they can reread their writing, like you are doing?"

Phrase your compliment in such a way that it doesn't simply name what the child did that day, but rather names work that the writer could apply to other texts. For example, if a child added into her draft the sound her guinea pig makes when it squeaks, you won't say, "I love that you added the /ē/ sound to your story. I hope you add that squeaking sound into your stories often!" Instead, you'll name what the child has done in a way that makes the action replicable: "I love the way you reread and added teeny details that could help readers create movies in their minds of exactly what happened. You made it so I can hear your guinea pig. Whenever you write, add details like these." Or "I love the way you've brought out dialogue—even if it is guinea-pig dialogue! You didn't just say, 'Freddy made noises to greet me'; you told us exactly what he said!"

In the compliment portion of a conference, then, you can forever alter a writer's sense of himself. You can help a writer recognize his talents and feel a sense of mission that comes from knowing one has gifts to give the world. You can remind the writer to use and develop and trust emerging talents and techniques, drawing on these often in future writing projects. You can make a writer aware of something he may have done accidentally, making it more likely that the writer does that again, with new deliberateness. That is gigantically important work.

> *In the compliment portion of a conference, you can forever alter a writer's sense of himself.*

Anthony Bryk, President of the Carnegie Foundation, once said that for an innovation to take hold in a school—and I believe this is also true for an innovation to take hold in a person's life—the participant needs to feel that the innovation fits her as a person, that it matches her identity. "This is my sort of thing," the learner needs to feel. "This fits me."

There are countless ways for writing to "fit" with a person. You can be a strong writer because you know that the details of your life and your thinking matter, and you bring them to the page. You can be a strong writer because you care about people and write with a consciousness of your readers and their questions. My point is that the writing workshop needs to be a place where there are lots of ways to be excellent, and where your kids know they are invited to bring their all to the work of making something beautiful.

Teach

The question is—how can you make the teaching portion of your conference matter to your students?

Know first that for a conference to matter, it helps if you aspire to teach in big and important ways that make a difference, not only to this day and this piece of writing,

but to the writer's work going forward. You are aiming to teach the writer, not the writing. Aim to go big. You are saying, "I think you are ready for gigantic, important new work." Martin Luther King, Jr. didn't say, "I have a plan for you." He said, "I have a dream." In the teach portion of a conference, expect to give a keynote, not merely to give a tip.

Choose a strategy or tip to teach that will help the child in lasting ways—one that sets up an industrious kind of work.

To teach the writer something enduring, the goal is not to assign the writer a five-minute task that she can do to improve the text. Instead, the goal is to help writers learn a concept, technique, tool, or strategy that they can draw on often.

Making Your Teaching Points Usable Again and Again

You could even be more ambitious, setting the writer up for days of work, by saying, "And Rachel, when you go to add the setting, you could just tell it straight out: 'We were at Lucky Strike Lanes.' But it is really, really great if you can show the setting. Maybe you say, 'The van pulled to a stop beside a huge glittering sign that said Lucky Strike Lanes.' And maybe there are other places throughout the story where you could add in a few lines that show what you were seeing. Remember, always, that good writers don't just tell the setting, they show it."

Then again, you could have amped up that conference in an entirely different way, saying, "And you know what? You can reread your writing for other elements of story as well. You know how in reading, you look at the problem in a story, and the way that problem gets worse and worse? You can reread your personal narratives and ask, 'Have I put forward a problem and shown the character resolving (or learning from) that problem?'"

If you find yourself about to give a tiny tip to a writer, think, "What is this tip an example of? What is the bigger principle I can teach?" For example, instead of suggesting that the writer merely tell what the father said, channel the writer to bring people to life by adding in what they said and thought and did. Instead of channeling the writer to add in a line indicating that the bowling party was at Lucky Strike Lanes, help the writer to study how another author wove the setting into many places in her story, and challenge your writer to do the same.

You may worry that you are asking too much—but if you think about the times when someone has helped you outgrow yourself in leaps and bounds, chances are that the person rallied you to tackle work that you feared was more than you could do. But that person saw more in you than you saw in yourself. That person probably communicated absolute faith in your ability to do big and important work, and that faith probably led you to work harder and to reach higher. Let that memory nudge you to be more ambitious for your youngsters.

Consider the teaching methods you'll use as you support the writer in trying the new work.

Finally, you'll want to think about your teaching methods during this teaching part of the conference. Will you demonstrate? Engage the child in guided practice? Provide an explanation and an example? Support the child in shared inquiry?

Sometimes, after offering a strategy, you can ask the writer to either go off on his own and try the strategy you've just described or get started trying to do that work right now, as you watch (and coach). Often, though, you'll need to give an example from your own work or even show the writer what this might look like in his own work. The point will be to use whatever you have on hand to demonstrate the step-by-step process that a writer goes through to use the strategy to reach the goal.

Sometimes, after you give a quick demonstration yourself or show a quick example, you'll want the student to try the work while you watch and coach. For example, imagine the writer of an information book has written only one sentence of information about each of her subtopics, and you've suggested that she could reread the piece and star places where she could say more. In this case, you might suggest she point to a place in the text where she plans to write more and say aloud what she plans to write. Or, if you decide the writer needs more support, you might say, "So let's try this together." Then you might read aloud the relevant portion of the writer's draft, leaving spaces for the writer to do the new work. After helping—scaffolding—in that way, you'd help the child go through the work again, this time relying on fewer scaffolds.

Link

After the writer has done a bit of the work on his or her own (even if that work occurs in the conference, with the benefit of your scaffolding), you will want to name what the writer has done that he or she can do so again within this draft and when working on other pieces of writing. The link is a time for you to channel writers to link what they've learned from you and begin applying it without your support. Usually this means the writer heads off to work on his or her own. Sometimes you weigh in after the writer has done that important work, in which you'll probably set the writer up to do similar work another time.

As part of this, it is not uncommon for you to repeat the teaching point, this time not as a charge to the writer, but as a record of what the writer has just done. As you remind the writer that it will be important to continue doing this good work often in future writing pieces, you'll explicitly support transference of what you have taught today into the child's ongoing independent writing process. Keep in mind the cardinal rule I described earlier: the challenge is to do all this, making sure the youngster's energy for writing goes up, not down. The writer should leave wanting to write.

Sources of Knowledge to Draw Upon When You Confer

In the conferring clinics that I described earlier, we ask teachers to help each other lift the level of their conferences. To do that, we ask the person who assumes the role of teacher in the conference to think aloud, and we ask the person functioning as the conferring coach to record the thinking that the teacher does. Then we ask teachers to notice what knowledge they tend to draw upon, what topics enter their mind, as they read and listen to the writer. Someone once said, "We do not see with our eyes or hear with our ears, but with our beliefs," and there is enormous truth to that. It is helpful to become more self-aware and to realize that we all tend to bring a few lenses to whatever we see and hear in a child's writing. Our teaching will be better if we learn to draw on as much knowledge as possible, including what we know about the qualities of good writing, the writing process, a particular child, mentor texts.

Your conferences will become better as you become more expert (as you develop more wisdom to draw upon in your conferences). They will also become better when you habitually draw on more sources of information.

FIG. 6–1 First-grader Arielle's Small Moment story shows a command of the genre by using a variety of details that bring her story to life.

Genre

Is it clear what genre the piece is intended to be? What are the main things that matter in that genre? More specifically, when thinking about one important dimension of the genre, what has this writer mastered and what seem like important next steps?

For example, perhaps this writer seems to be attempting to write an opinion piece. It might be a review of a favorite pizza restaurant. The writer has named her opinion. "Bob's Pizza is GREAT." She has named a reason that she loves the place ("The pizza is delicious!") and she says more about that reason ("The cheese is gooey and tasty."). She doesn't yet, however, know that she is expected to provide another reason or two to support her claim.

Content

Does it seem as if the writer is deeply committed to the content? Often it's the writer's absorption in the content that engages the reader in the content. If this is a story, is one able to read the text and experience the events, as if these are real? Where does the reader's experience fall apart? If this is an expository text, is the reader able to learn from it? Where does that learning happen easily and where does it fall apart? Or, in an opinion/argument text, is the reader persuaded? What feels untrue or off-track and what can the writer do about it? What feels important, beautiful, or new to the writer and how can that be developed?

Lifting the Writing Process with a Focus on Students' Strengths

Work with the writer's strengths. For example, learn whether these writers . . .

- consider their lives to be a source of ideas, readily coming up with ideas for what to write about.

- have ways of getting started, such as touching each page and saying what they'll write.

- have a sense of the tools they'll need, such as flaps for adding on as they revise.

- think about the genre, saying things like "I need to tell what happens at the end."

And when thinking about revising, do writers . . .

- make larger revisions, such as adding (or taking out) whole sentences, or sometimes even whole parts?

- use revision tools to support the work, such as flaps, strips, and colored pens?

- return to many pages and even many pieces of writing to apply a revision strategy, rather than only revising one page?

- revise with an increasing sense of purpose, considering the effect that this or that choice will have on readers?

Engagement

As you progress through your conference, you'll also want to keep tabs on the writer's energy and openness. Be ready to moderate what you say in an effort to recruit the writer's attention and to rally the writer's zeal. Note instances when a writer's zeal for writing increases, and let that response inform your teaching. Notice, too, times when the writer seems to shrink in front of you, to be less full of himself or herself. There's your feedback! This pressure to respond to the writer will spur you to be inventive.

With Whom Will You Confer?

Although the context for your conferences will be created by the entire fabric of your teaching, conferring itself creates its own organizational challenges. For example, you will need to decide how you'll figure out which child to meet with next. Teachers develop their own idiosyncratic systems for this. Some teachers enter a writing workshop with a little list in hand of writers they plan to see. The list may come from studying assessments of students or from conferring/small-group records indicating children who have and haven't yet received feedback. The list may also come from thinking about previous conferences that need follow-up. Or it may come from thinking about or reading through children's work and deciding on those who need help and those who could, with help, do exemplary work that might fuel the next minilesson, mid-workshop teaching, or share.

Personally, although I do enter a workshop with a list of the children with whom I hope to confer, I find it is important to improvise based on the signals children give me. That is, if youngsters at one table seem unsettled, I'm apt to confer with a child at that table, knowing that my presence can channel the entire group to work rather than socialize. Then, too, if one child is especially persistent about needing help, I generally make that child a priority—unless he is always at my elbow; in which case, I'll respond differently.

I tell children that if they need my help, they should get out of their seats and follow me as I confer. I find this keeps the child who feels stymied from derailing her companions as well; in addition, the children learn from eavesdropping on conferences. The line that forms behind me also provides me with a very tangible reminder of how many children feel confused or stuck at any moment, and this keeps me on my toes. If I have six children in tow, I'm not apt to overlook them for long.

Keep Conference Records

You will definitely want to record your conferences and small-group work, and to develop a system for doing so that fits into the rhythms of your own teaching. The important thing is that the writing about teaching that you do must help you teach better and help your students learn better. This writing needs to be attuned to your teaching, reflecting, and planning. You will probably go through a sequence of systems before settling, temporarily, on one.

Many teachers keep a page on a clipboard that looks like a month-at-a-glance calendar but is, instead, the class-at-a-glance. For the period of time this page represents (which tends to be two weeks), the teacher records the compliment and teaching point of most conferences. On the other hand, some teachers create a record-keeping sheet that culls some main goals from the learning progression for the type of writing they're teaching. They record their observations of children's work on that sheet, essentially saying that this particular child is working toward this sticky note on the anchor chart, and that child, toward this other one.

Some teachers have notebooks divided into sections, one for each child, and record their conferences with each child that way. Others do a variation of this, recording the conferences on large sticky notes and later moving the notes to the appropriate section of the notebook. Some record conferences in the student's writing folder, allowing them to look at both the notes from prior conferences and the child's work when in a conference.

Of course, many teachers prefer to keep digital conference notes. Applications, such as Evernote, that allow users to create, tag, and sort notes are a favorite with writing workshop teachers. Many of these applications have photo and video functionality, so that you can add photos of kids' work or audio recordings of conferences to their notes.

In Evernote, you can create a separate digital notebook for each child, so that each child's conferences are grouped together and you can quickly scan all of the kinds of conferences you do with that child. You can also tag each note with descriptors that indicate the content of the conference, making it easy to sort across your class list to find students who had similar conferences. For example, you could use a tag like *setting* to indicate all of the students with whom you'd conferred about setting, and you could use that information to plan next steps for these students in a small group, or to identify which students hadn't yet had this kind of conference.

Working with Classroom Volunteers

Occasionally, you might have adults, such as specialists, teaching assistants, student teachers, or family volunteers, who join your writing workshop to confer with students. If so, the tips below can guide these helpers to confer in ways that lift students' work, even if they are not trained in writing-workshop teaching methods.

Conferring Successfully

- Work with a student for a short period—about five minutes. This way, the student gets support and also has plenty of time to work independently.

- Children are working at their own pace and may be in different stages of the writing process. To work with them most effectively, it helps to consider where in the process they are: are they coming up with a topic, planning, writing, revising, or editing? Help the writer with his or her stage of the writing process.

- In writing workshop, we coach kids to use their phonics knowledge to spell words. This means kids' writing will include approximated spellings, as kids write words they know but can't yet spell conventionally. Coach kids to draw on all their phonics knowledge and strategies they know to approximate spelling, and then to keep going.

- Teachers typically do not write on student pieces. If you would like to leave a quick reminder, you can jot something on a sticky note and leave that behind. It's helpful to carry tools, such as sticky notes, blank paper and pens, and a whiteboard and markers, in case you want to show a student something.

In Closing

When you watch a very skilled writing teacher confer, it can seem as if she pulled the perfect conference out of thin air—but you need to know that her skill comes from a great deal of practice and from deep knowledge. With practice and time, you'll get there too. You'd be wise to fill yourself with images of the look, sound, and feel of effective writing conferences. Watch video clips of conferences, and visit schools where teachers have received professional development in conferring. Study the conferences across the *Supporting All Writers: High-Leverage Small Groups and Conferences, K–2.* Doing so can deepen your understanding of how writing conferences can go and can broaden your repertoire of ready-to-go conferences. It will also help you to work with a colleague to develop the thinking part of your conferences. Look at a student's writing together and talk about what you notice. Your conferring will get better if you are able to notice more (or different aspects) of the student's writing and to draw on more wisdom about qualities of good writing.

Finally, as I said at the start of this chapter, remember times when people have observed your work and then spoken to you about it in ways that made a world of difference. Draw on your memories of what you, as a learner, have needed. Remember that your feedback can make a world of difference.

Small-Group Work in the Writing Workshop

7

Small-Group Work in the Writing Workshop

Rufus Jones, the great American Quaker, once said, "I pin my hopes on the quiet processes and small circles in which vital and transforming change take place." Margaret Mead put it this way: "Never doubt that a small group of thoughtful, committed citizens can change the world; indeed, it is the only thing that ever has."

I've cited those quotes often when talking to teachers and school leaders about the importance of creating a collaborative learning community among the professionals in a school. I've often told them that the best thing about adopting a workshop approach to teaching writing is that this brings teachers together into the small study groups that vitalize the learning culture in a school.

Whenever teachers visit schools that are TCRWP strongholds, I try to make sure they are able to visit not only the classrooms, but also the study groups for teachers across grade levels. I'll take visitors in to see a group of teachers—say, six second-grade teachers—working together to make teaching tools, role-playing responses to student work, puzzling over how to teach a particularly challenging concept. After observing such a study group for five or ten minutes, the visitors and I will pull into the corridor and I'll explain: "The study group you just watched is the way that this school lifts the level of everyone's teaching. The more experienced teachers end up supporting the newer teachers, and everyone gets opportunities to reflect and practice with the support of others."

Recently, my colleagues and I have realized that we don't usually think of the small groups we lead for children in similar ways—and we should. The opportunity to learn alongside a small group of one's peers can matter as much to kids as it matters to us. These small groups give kids the chance to try something new with the support of one another. When kids who are ready to try something new or challenging can work in pairs, first on one child's draft and then on the other's, this social support is a critical structure. Small groups also provide us as teachers with ways to be more efficient in our teaching. Instead of teaching lessons and sharing tips with one child after another, we teach several children in concert. This allows five minutes of our teaching time to support half a dozen kids instead of just one child, as in a conference.

Small-Group Examples

There are several ways small groups usually go. This repertoire of ways small groups can go allows you to adjust your teaching in response to your students.

Revising Dialogue Using a "Friend's" Demonstration for Practice

Picture a group of second-graders in a narrative unit of study who are writing streams of dialogue, interspersed with very few speech tags or intervening actions. Their pieces go something like this:

> Basketball
>
> "You guys wanna play some ball?" "Sure." "Three on three." "Hey, pass to me, I'm open!" "Heads up Tyson." "Hey, I was open." "That was a foul."

You gather the students and tell them why you pulled them together. You'll tell them what they are doing that works well, and then you also tell them what they could be doing but aren't yet doing. "I gathered you because you are all getting the people in your stories to talk, which is great. Congratulations for that! When I read your writing, I can hear it. Your writing is the soundtrack to a movie." Continuing, you say, "That made me realize you are ready for the next step. What I want to teach you today is that neither a movie nor a story can be just a soundtrack, just what you hear. The movie also needs the part that you see, the part that includes the actions that the people are doing."

> *Small groups provide kids with the social support, the company, that they need to try something just a notch challenging for them.*

Then you can ask each pair of kids to look at the writing one of them did, helping that writer to add in who was talking and what the person was doing. To scaffold this work, you might create an intermediary step, telling the small group that you have a neighbor who came by last night, wanting help—and you wonder if they could help that neighbor by showing her how she can revise her text so it is not just a soundtrack. That piece might be just two or three sentences long—and easily fixed. To keep this work brief, you might even suggest the partners just write the imagined text "in the air." The draft, ostensibly written by the neighbor, is ideally part of a toolkit of resources that you draw on repeatedly. That is, often when kids need support, it is helpful for us to write an exercise text, a super-brief text, copies of which can be given to several partnerships at the same time. These texts set kids up to do the work that their own writing requires, but in the text you create for this purpose, the need for that work and the way to pull it off can be especially obvious.

Initial Draft

> Swimming
>
> "Hold me hold me. I might drown."
>
> "I got you." "Please don't drop me."
>
> "I'm not gonna drop you. Just kick."

Revised Draft

> Swimming
>
> "Hold me, hold me, I might drown," I said. I was in the pool and my sister was holding me up. "I got you," my sister said. "Please don't drop me." I answered and I grabbed my sister's arm.
>
> "I'm not gonna drop you! Just kick."

Coaching Moves for Revising Writing

After kids work on the "practice text," you channel them to do similar work on their work—doing it collaboratively. As the kids work with first one writer's text and then the other's, you might coach:

- "Try making a movie in your mind of what happened. What exactly were you doing?"
- "What exactly? Can you think of the smaller action?"
- "Reread what you've written, seeing if this makes sense and if you can picture it."
- "You might need to add in, 'I said.' Help readers know who is talking."
- "Pretend you are a stranger to this writing. Read it over and check that it makes sense."
- "Don't forget you know how to spell your snap words in a snap! The word wall can help."

After kids work on this, you could suggest they each reread their earlier stories to find others that needed similar attention. "When you get back to your seat, you might revise another one of your stories. Or just get started writing some new stories, but remember: dialogue, action, dialogue, action."

Revising to Make Writing More Readable

Let's look at another exemplar small group. Picture a group of kindergartners in a narrative unit of study who are making good attempts to capture all the sounds they hear in words and to record multiple words on a page. However, their writing appears as strings of letters, difficult to read or interpret.

Their pieces look something like those in Figure 7–1.

You gather the students and explain why you pulled them together. You tell them what they are doing well and then explain what you'd like to help them do next. "I gathered you all because you are hearing so many sounds in words, and you are working so hard to get all of those sounds on the page. So you tell a story. Well done!"

Continuing, you say, "You are ready for the next step." Here, you might give a little example, before segueing to your teaching point, "You know how sometimes the TV gets all staticky and hard to hear? The picture is easy to see, but the words are hard to understand. It's hard to tell what's happening. Sometimes writing ends up like that, all staticky. Sometimes the words are not so clear, and it's hard to understand the story."

Then you distribute two pieces of writing to each partnership (see Figures 7–1 and 7–2). Note that one of the pieces will look similar to the kind of work the kids are now doing, and the other will be an improved version of the same story, showing the kind of work you hope they will do next.

Invite partners to study the two pieces with each other, naming what the writer did to make the second version much more readable. Coach children as they talk with their partner. You might join one partnership to share your own noticing. The writer fixed the first story up by using spaces between words, recording more sounds in words, spelling snap words correctly, and so forth. As children talk, use what you hear them saying to annotate the second piece with sticky notes that label the work the writers have done: hears more sounds, uses a period. You are creating an exemplar, using their observations. Of course, you may need to do some translating as you record what they say so that the language is clearer.

Next, channel children to their own writing. Ask them to take out the piece they are currently working on and to continue where they left off—this time aiming to do the things they noticed in the exemplar to make their writing more readable. As they write, rotate among them, coaching with lean prompts, pointing to the exemplar, giving reminders. After they've written a page or so, ask them to pause and reread their writing as a way to check their work. Support them in fixing up their writing as needed. You might then leave the children working, perhaps huddled around the marked-up exemplar for continued support. Remind them to aim for these ways to make their writing more readable each time they write.

FIG. 7–1 Version 1

FIG. 7–2 Version 2

Unpacking the Exemplars: Big Ideas about Small Groups

So what are the implications of these examples of how small groups might go in the classroom? In small groups, kids work together to take their writing up a notch, to get better at applying all they've already been taught. This is usually a time to work on the hard parts of something related to their ongoing work. Occasionally, this is a time to suggest a new horizon for kids who are eager for a next step beyond what the class has been studying.

Begin by giving a purpose.

The small group usually begins with you telling kids why you called them together, usually by naming what the group has already been able to do and explaining there is a next step for them to work on together. You set them up to get started. This takes about a minute, total.

Writers work together.

The bulk of the group time is devoted to kids doing something with each other, usually working in pairs (usually these are writing partners) and sometimes starting by working on one person's draft, then working on the other's draft. Sometimes the work is done on an exercise text or a mentor text. This portion of the small group is usually divided into two "try its," or two activities, with the first being far more accessible than the second. Perhaps the first "try it" engages both partnerships in talking through the bullets of an anchor chart, telling each other whether they often or rarely do each bullet, one by one. Then the second "try it" asks more of children. Perhaps the partners decide on one item from the anchor chart that they both have done rarely, and now the two of them help one of them do that work. They may or may not work on the second child's text.

Coach in to lift the level of work.

As kids work, you listen, expecting the kids to approximate. You do not intervene to make the work correct or perfect, but instead you intervene with coaching prompts that aim to lift the level of the kids' work. Your coaching tends to be sentence-long prompts, rather than full conversations.

Writers complete series of activities.

For example, kids might first annotate a mentor text by applying the points on a checklist to the mentor text. Then they might try to annotate their own writing using similar tags. Or they might first point at the people in their story and say aloud what each person might be saying. Then they might attempt to write this dialogue either as speech bubbles in their picture or integrated into their lines of text, or both. You may leave in the midst of this work to support other children, leaving group members to help one another.

Wrap up and extend learning.

The group usually ends with you channeling kids to apply what they have learned to their own writing. You often emphasize that what they have learned is for every day, every piece, not just for this piece and this day.

SMALL GROUP ✦ Finding Fix-Up Spots, and Fixing Them Up!

For this small group, you'll need copies of Gerty's writing, "The Writing Center," one per partnership.

■ **RALLY**

Suggest that writers look closely and find more things to fix. Brainstorm and list things they can look for when editing.

"Writers, some of you are finding just one thing to fix up on each page of your writing. We've been looking closely at lots of different things in this unit. I think we can do the same in our writing, and find lots of things to fix up.

"Let's make a list of things to check for. You say them, and I'll write them on this white-board!" Students' list included: capitals, periods, exclamation points, question marks, snap words, missing words.

■ **TRY IT #1**

Ask students to help you do this work on your neighbor Gerty's writing.

"My neighbor, Gerty, brought me her writing. She wants your help fixing it up! Read her writing, and if you notice anything that needs fixing, jump in and help her."

■ **TRY IT #2**

Ask students to switch pieces and count the number of fix-its needed. Then have them switch back and try to fix up those places.

"Sometimes it's easier to see fix-ups in another writer's writing, just like we did with Gerty's writing. Gerty doesn't have her own writing partner, but you do! Swap your writing with your partner and read. If you see a fix-up that is needed, leave a tiny pencil dot in that place. Remember, look for things like snap words that need to be fixed up, missing punctuation, and even places where your partner needs to add a word or take a word out. When you're done, give the book back to the writer, and writers, go ahead and fix those things up!"

■ **LINK**

Celebrate how writers fixed up their writing. Encourage partners to try this work moving forward.

"Wow, writers! You found so many places to fix up! From now on, try to read super-closely when you're looking for fix-up spots, and know you can use a partner to help you see more."

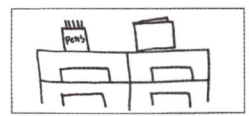

> The writing center haz
> Many things It haz pens,
> paper, and revision flaps.
> in writing workshop you
> can tak what you need
> you need It

> the paper in the writing
> center Iz different some
> hav a lot of lins. It Is fun
> to pick!

Gerty's writing

Possible Coaching Moves:

▸ *"Check for words you know in a snap!"*

▸ *"Reread this part again. Does this sound like how a book would talk?"*

▸ *"Talk with your partner if you can't find all the fix-its."*

This small group, from Grade 1, Unit 2, can be found in the online resources.

The Architecture of a Small Group

Most small groups in both reading and writing follow a similar architecture. These are exceptions, but the small group on the previous page is very representative. The entire group, with all these parts, generally lasts five-to-seven minutes.

Rally

You convey the reason for the teaching that you are about to do, building students' commitment to the work and their sense of how it will fit with their ongoing work. Think of this as your opportunity to give the tiniest keynote imaginable, in just a few sentences. For instance, if you gathered a group of students who needed to remember to use the correct vowel when writing, you might start the group by saying, "Writers, I know you've been studying vowel power during phonics time. But here's the thing. Vowel power is also super-important when you write because every word needs at least one vowel. When you want to say, 'I'll give you a hat,' you wouldn't want to mix up the vowels and accidentally say, 'I'll give you a hit!'"

As you rally kids to the work of the group, you might briefly activate their prior knowledge, reminding them of something they've been taught but may not yet be drawing on automatically. Usually to do that, you give each partnership a familiar chart to hold and review. You might say, "Will you read over this chart to review your vowels? Come up with some words for each vowel." Sometimes this work is actually "Try It #1."

Try It #1

In most small groups, you provide students two opportunities to practice the skill or strategy you are teaching or reviewing. For their first try, you channel students to do this work in a very accessible way. Students usually do the work in partnerships. If you are supporting kids with vowel power as in the example above, you might give each partnership a pile of objects and ask them to name the object and agree on the vowel in the object's name.

Sometimes, you will channel kids to do a bit of very supported work on a very brief text that you claim was written by another student or your neighbor. In these instances, you produce a very short text that is riddled with the kinds of challenges you're seeing in the kids' writing. Partners reread the writing done by that imaginary writer, working together to help that writer in ways that they'll soon need to do in their own writing.

Coaching Prompts that Support Writers

- "Do that again!"
- "Do you want an example? Ask your partner for one."
- "Check this one. See if it makes sense."
- "Reread and see if your writing is easy to read. Fix it up if not."
- "Is there a different way you could try that?"
- "Check for spaces between your words."
- "I find that a little confusing. Ask your partner to explain."
- "Check your work with each other."

Coach

As kids work, you'll coach them. Think of your coaching as lean prompts as well as next-step direction that combine to keep children working or talking with each other. Your coaching doesn't involve a back-and-forth conversation. You often coach the listening partner by saying, "Ask your partner to say more." "Do you want to hear another example? Tell her." You might coach the whole group. "When you finish one, go to the next." You are nudging the work the kids are doing to ratchet it up just a notch.

Try It #2

If your first activity was easy for kids, this one steps things up. This may be harder work or may decrease scaffolding. Often, in this portion, you invite kids to do the work now that they tried on a practice text in their own writing, working in pairs to help each other do this. If the small group involved kids in helping an imaginary neighbor check their writing to be sure she included a vowel in every syllable, this is the time either each of your children would check their own writing or they'd work in pairs to help each other.

If the children have been revising the heart of their story by acting it out and then writing it bit by bit, this might be a time when they reread other stories they have written to find another that merits similar revision work. The idea is that kids will benefit from repeated practice of whatever it is you prompted them to do earlier.

We recommend having children usually work in pairs, which allows you to listen in on their work, shifting your attention efficiently from one pair of children to another and coaching based on what you hear.

Link

This section of a small group is a lot like the link at the end of your minilessons. This is your opportunity to remind students of what they've learned and to set them up to continue applying the focus principle to their ongoing writing work. If students just edited a neighbor's writing for short vowels, you might say, "Writers, what you did to help my neighbor with her writing should help you with your writing—today and every day. You'll see I've marked a page of your writing with a pink sticky note. Before you continue with today's writing, will you reread that page, checking that you've included short vowels when needed? You'll need to do a bit of fixing up. Then continue your writing, but keep these tricky short vowels in mind as you work."

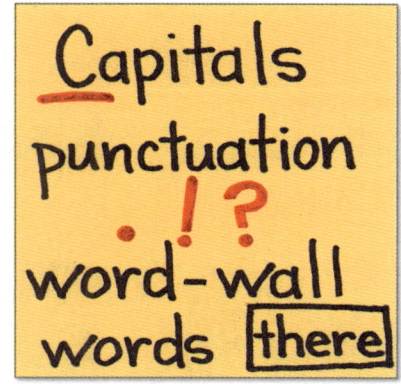

Artifacts like sticky notes can help writers remember a lesson during future work.

One way to increase the likelihood that the work kids do in a small group makes a lasting impact is if you leave an artifact for them to keep after the group is over, such as a reminder sticky note or a mini-chart.

A Final Word about Small-Group Work

The evolution of the small group to its current form took time and careful consideration, and there are lessons to be learned from the history of this element of the writing workshop model.

Small Groups Are Not Minilessons

There was a time when my colleagues and I imagined small groups as miniature workshops, complete with a tiny minilesson and then some work time and then a share. That didn't work well for a number of reasons. First, the burden of planning was just too much. Those small groups required so much preparation that most teachers shied away from them. Then, too, the net effect was that some kids sat through a too-long minilesson followed by a too-long small group. And when the teacher worked one-to-one with each writer in the group, the other writers tended to just sit and stare, waiting for their turn in the teacher's successive conversations. We've become convinced that small groups fulfill a very different function than minilessons and that they are nothing like miniature minilessons.

In small groups, the priority needs to be for children to be active and interactive and for you to listen and coach. Your direct talking to kids might occupy 5% of the total time in a small group, but no more. The goal is for learners to work collaboratively to do something they wouldn't have done without your nudge, while you shift between observing and coaching.

Small Groups Offer the Opportunity to Apply Skills

Most small groups aren't teaching brand-new content. That content already comes at kids fast and furious. The last thing kids need is to go from a minilesson to a small group in which we throw a whole new raft of teaching points at them. The hard part about learning to write is not hearing tips—it is actually employing those tips in the context of one's writing. So if you find that in your small groups you regularly toss new tools and techniques at your kids, consider instead giving them time and support to "own" the tools and techniques they already have in hand.

For example, you might simply show some writers a familiar chart and ask them to talk in twos about which strategies on that chart they use regularly and which they rarely use. Then you might ask them to choose a strategy they rarely use and to help each partner in turn use that strategy in her writing. Voilà! A very effective small group. The book *Supporting All Writers: High-Leverage Small Groups and Conferences, K–2* will allow you to imagine a way to teach almost any concept in a more rudimentary form. If you have some second-graders who are struggling with transitions, that book will show you ways to teach this same concept to less experienced writers. That is, the volume will add enormous scope to your teaching.

Learning to write is not all that different from learning to play tennis or any other sport. When I'm trying to play tennis, I already know in my head a score of things that I don't yet know in my body. People can tell me, "Follow through on your strokes." I get it. I've heard that before. I just somehow am not yet doing it, and I'm especially not doing that when things get heated. What I need are opportunities for repeated practice. I may even need some success and for that, I may need my coach to send some easier serves my way—ones that arrive right where my racket is—so that I can focus less on running for the ball and more on following through with my stroke. Kids' needs aren't any different. There are lots and lots of things they've already been taught to do that they need support in actually doing, again and again, with increasing finesse.

Small Groups Can Employ Familiar Tools

I worry that teachers have been made to feel that you need to prepare for small groups by bringing stuff to the kids: fancy new charts, sheets with steps listed. "I don't want to go into a small group and feel empty-handed," teachers tell me. Perhaps you can relate to that feeling. But the truth is that you'd lead a perfectly good small group by bringing a chart from your phonics or your reading instruction to kids and suggesting that they examine their writing to see ways they are—and aren't yet—using what they know about phonics or reading as they write. That is, you do not need endless charts and tools to support small groups. In fact, it's almost a disservice to use tools that are disconnected from your kids' work and from your curriculum. Instead, your small groups should become a time to help your kids actually use what they have learned. Yes, you'll want to give them a few visuals to help them transfer what they do in the small group to their everyday writing. For the most part, however, these will be the charts, tips checklists, and mentor texts that you've already brought to your kids during minilessons.

Small Groups Can Target Kids' Next Steps

Sometimes, the small groups we teach feel out of reach for the writers we've gathered together, and we end up providing tons of scaffolding, demonstrations, and tools—even doing the work for the kids so that the small group feels successful. Instead, what I suggest is that you teach small groups that represent a next-step forward for your writers, one that is well within their zone of proximal development.

In addition to the small groups in your units of study books, *Supporting All Writers: High-Leverage Small Groups and Conferences*, K–2 will be an important support as you identify next steps for your students. Inside the book, you'll find a series of progressions that can help you pinpoint the next steps that can help writers with any particular skill. For instance, if you're teaching students to add on to their opinion writing, you might turn to the "Saying More about Your Opinions" progression and study the strategies, noting which will provide an appropriate next step for your writers. Perhaps your writers need to first add details to their pictures, before they are ready to add details to their words. Maybe your writers are ready to add on using examples or evidence from a text. Or you might even have writers who are ready to craft stories to add to their opinion writing. Wherever your writers are, *Supporting All Writers: High-Leverage Small Groups and Conferences*, K–2 will guide you to pinpoint powerful next steps that will accelerate your children's writing development.

Center the Students' Work with Each Other

The other important thing to remember is that you will want to do everything possible to decentralize small groups so that children can work with each other, not relying on you. To keep your children relying on and helping each other, allow them to work as best they can, imperfectly. That is, if the activity you imagine involves two children annotating a mentor text with the qualities of good writing they note in that text, you'll need to expect that they will only do that work as best they can.

Although it may be tempting to intercede whenever you see an error, remember that approximation is how people learn. Think back to the tennis example, and think about how children learn to play a sport or musical instrument. There will inevitably be a lot of imperfect work along those learning pathways, and learning anything in literacy will be no different. Small groups provide an opportunity for your students to learn from each other and benefit from each other's example, with a little guidance to nudge them toward greater proficiency and independence. Your kids need to be active and interactive so you can observe and coach. The key thing to remember is that you'll coach into their work in ways that lead not to correctness necessarily, but to continual improvement.

Although there will be times when you lead small-group work to address youngsters who have specific needs that aren't being met by the curriculum alone, it's important that all your small groups are not designed for kids who need to catch up. Think of the message you'd send if all your small groups were designed to address problems. A child would approach such a group as if he had been sent to the principal's office! All students deserve instruction, and many of your small groups will be equally valuable to any writer. For example, if you planned a small group to help children develop the setting in their stories, you could simply ask, "Would some of you like to make your stories even better?" and then help the writers who volunteer for this important (and fun) work.

> *You will want to do everything possible to decentralize small groups so that children can work with each other, not relying on you.*

The goal is to accelerate each child's learning and to give each child an education aligned to that child's particular, individual ways of representing knowledge and of engaging with texts.

Affirming and Supporting Multilingual Language Learners

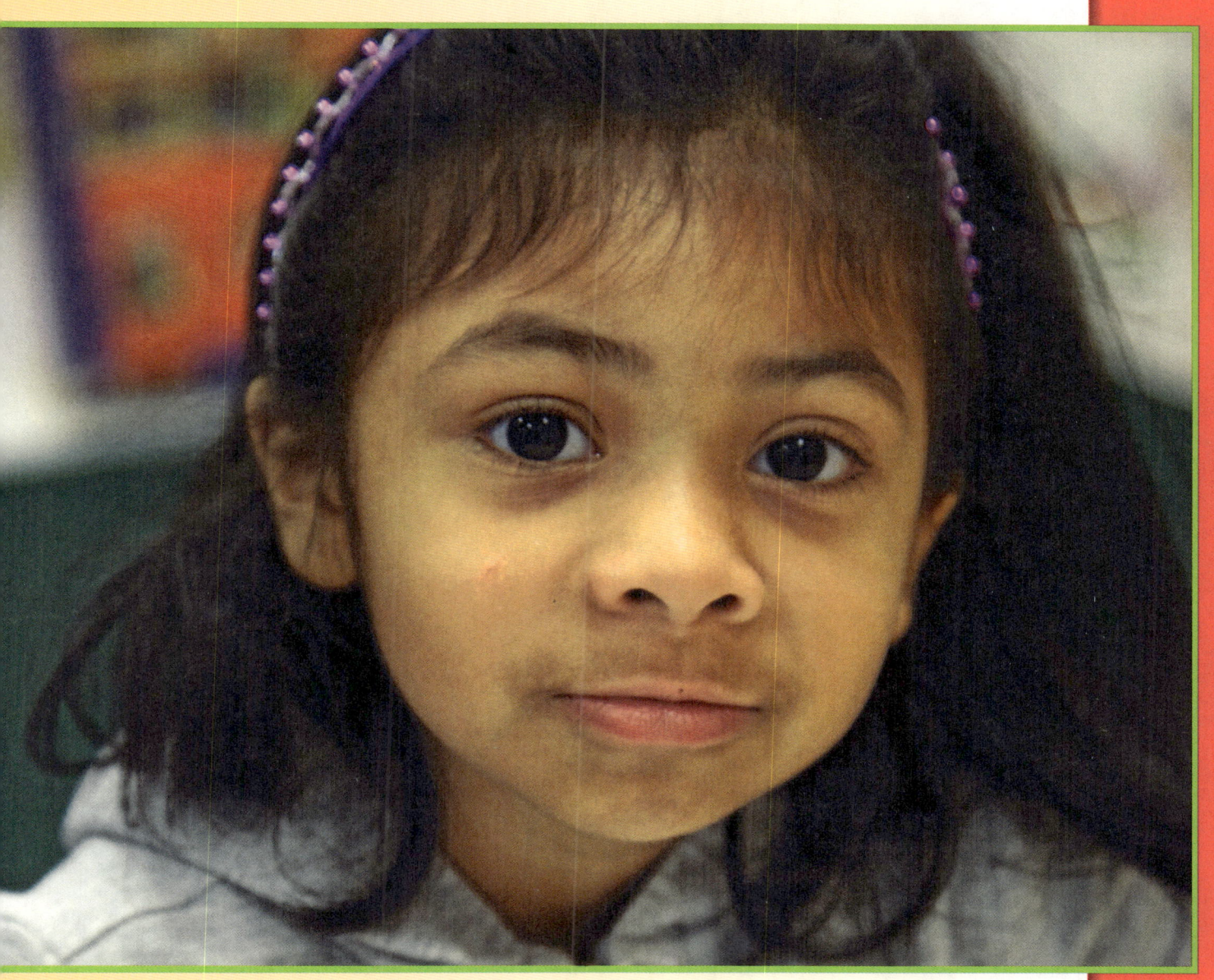

8

Affirming and Supporting Multilingual Language Learners

Because the TCRWP is deeply involved with schools where classrooms brim with multilingual language learners (MLLs), we spend a lot of time thinking about ways the reading and the writing workshops can help our MLLs to thrive. In many of our schools, teachers, coaches, and administrators have been working for decades teach writing and language simultaneously through writing workshops.

Research-Based Instruction

In 2021, a study of TCRWP by the American Institutes for Research (AIR) looked at the impact of teaching the Units of Study with fidelity in schools with a high percentage of students who were English learners. AIR's analysis found statistically significant gains made by all sectors of the population, including multilingual language learners, particularly in schools where the Units of Study had been taught across several years.

The last two decades have seen an explosion of research on the benefits of the bilingual brain, affirming the cognitive flexibility and improved problem-solving capacities demonstrated by multilingual language learners. Ever since Norma González, Luis Moll, and Cathy Amanti (2009) published the "funds of knowledge" theory, educators have urged all of us to focus on multilingual language learners' strengths—that is, to build on what multilingual language learners have already learned and experienced—as opposed to focusing on what are perceived weaknesses.

An Asset-Based Approach

What does it mean to bring an asset-based approach to your teaching? In part, this means expecting all your learners to thrive. If some students do not respond to your teaching, ask yourself, "How have I neglected to give these learners the conditions they need to thrive?" To establish asset-based learning environments, you'll also need to create a classroom community characterized by a commitment to coalition rather than competition. And you'll need to take on the work of coming to know each of your students individually.

For students to learn well, it is important that they bring their full selves to the classroom. One way to support that is by encouraging your students to draw on their personal lives and interests in the topics they write about and the audiences they write for. Zaretta Hammond's (2014) advice in *Culturally Responsive Teaching and The Brain* is wise. She points out that, yes, it is important to get to know the observable patterns in a child's culture—the clothes, foods, games, and holidays—but it is also important to understand the deep culture, which includes understanding the unspoken rules and norms around everyday social interactions and the assumptions that govern a family's worldview.

Assessment Formed through Strong Relationships

The word *assessment* doesn't do justice to the listening and learning you need to do to be ready to teach the children in your classroom who are English learners. You will need to quickly develop bonds with their families and their communities, learning about the languages they and their families speak, the passions and interests and traditions and literary texts in which they are immersed. Approach that study with appreciation and with a readiness to be a learner of language and culture yourself.

Be absolutely clear from the start that the language learners in your care will be very different, one from another. You need to build a relationship with each one, one by one. Each will bring a complex, beautiful tapestry of culture and language, dreams and ambitions, and, yes, anxieties and fears too.

> *You need to build a relationship with each language learner, one by one. Each will bring a complex, beautiful tapestry of culture and language, dreams and ambitions, and, yes, anxieties and fears too.*

Using Resources to Adapt Your Workshop

Chapter 9, "Ensuring Access," in combination with this chapter, will help you learn ways to adapt your writing workshop to be sure that you give all your students access to the richest possible instruction. We acknowledge that many of you teach children who speak dozens, even scores, of languages and wish that we were able, at this time, to provide you with resources to support all those language speakers. For now, we have been able to incorporate tools that have been translated into Spanish into the Units of Study in Writing and we've recommended Spanish books that are aligned to the curriculum. We've also filmed brief previews of every minilesson in Spanish. We hope that over time these supports will be available in other languages as well.

Supports for Multilingual Language Learners in Units of Study in Writing

- Every chart as well as every teaching point has been translated into Spanish.

- For every unit, there are suggested titles in Spanish. These are sometimes translations of the mentor texts and sometimes original Spanish texts. You'll want to check the online resources for the most up-to-date recommendations for Spanish mentor texts.

- For every minilesson, we've created a brief—two-minute—video preview in Spanish that sets up Spanish-speaking multilingual language learners to anticipate what they'll be learning in the minilesson. Each video unpacks key vocabulary, provides learners with helpful background knowledge, and explains any important metaphors used in the minilesson. Learners also get a glimpse into what the work they do during work time might look like. The videos have been designed so that children can easily access them while you are orchestrating whole-class transitions to the minilesson.

- Coaching tips throughout the sessions suggest ways the teaching is already supportive of English learners and additional ways to make your teaching even more supportive.

- Some work-time sessions are specifically designed to support your small-group work and conferring with multilingual language learners.

- Every session begins with an "Ensuring Access" section highlighting the essential goals of a session and detailing ways in which the session already provides access or can be taught in ways that especially do so.

- The writing workshop and, indeed, the entire school day immerse children in that sea of language that is incredibly supportive of MLLs' oral language development.

- Throughout the units, you'll support children in using all their language resources to mull over complicated ideas, rehearse for writing, and clarify their understanding of instruction and texts. We encourage you to allow children who need to do so to translanguage with each other in ways that help with their overall learning. You'll especially see children encouraged to rehearse for writing in whatever language they choose.

Our main priority when authoring the revision for this series has been to support teaching that is asset based, responsive, and respectful of each child's genius and each child's culture, language, and dreams. This should be evident throughout the series.

Ways the Materials and Structure of a Writing Workshop Can Support MLLs

Finding Mentor Texts in the Languages Your Children Know Best
Finding Mirrors and Windows for Every Child

You'll want to go to great lengths to provide your children with mentor texts in the languages they know best and to help them know many different authors. You'll see that the new Units of Study highlight many books that can serve as mirrors for children who are from groups that have been historically underrepresented in children's literature. Multilingual language learners often belong to these groups.

In her 2016 TED Talk, "The Windows and Mirrors of Your Child's Bookshelf," Grace Lin explained that when she was growing up, she never saw herself in the books that her teachers read or in the books she was given to read. The stories were always written by white authors, and they featured white characters. This experience, she said, made her want to forget that she was Asian. She described how the single book she was exposed to in elementary school that featured Asian characters was *The Five Chinese Brothers*

by Claire Huchet Bishop and Kurt Wiese. When her classmates compared Grace to the characters in that book, Grace felt "horrified by her own reflection in a mirror." This was one of the experiences that led Grace to create books that celebrate Asian culture and to create characters who serve as proud mirrors for Asian youngsters and celebratory windows for others.

The Power of Translanguaging

Make an extra effort to include books where the author chooses to translanguage. My colleague, the bilingual researcher Ofelia Garcia, has helped those of us who are monolingual become more aware of the power of translanguaging in the lives of our multilingual students. She writes, "If you've ever been present in the home of a

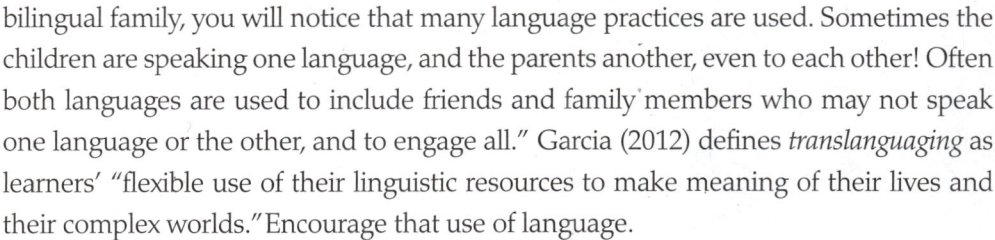

bilingual family, you will notice that many language practices are used. Sometimes the children are speaking one language, and the parents another, even to each other! Often both languages are used to include friends and family members who may not speak one language or the other, and to engage all." Garcia (2012) defines *translanguaging* as learners' "flexible use of their linguistic resources to make meaning of their lives and their complex worlds." Encourage that use of language.

You might, for example, show children Saadia Faruqi's book, *Yasmin the Teacher*, which is mostly written in English but includes words in Urdu as well. It is helpful for children to see that published authors sometimes decide the best way to communicate a meaning is by using another language. Teach your children that if, for example, a child's grandmother has a particular endearment she uses and she speaks in a language other than English, including her exact words in her true language will help the character come to life on the page.

Mentor Texts in Spanish

For students who read and write in Spanish, we've provided suggestions for Spanish mentor texts that you can incorporate into each writing unit. Some of these are authentic

Spanish texts, and others are translations. You'll want to check the online resources for the most up-to-date recommendations for Spanish mentor texts. 🖐

Using the Structure of Your Workshop to Support Your MLLs

A Predictable Structure

The good news is that the structure of the writing workshop and its sister, the reading workshop, is deliberately kept simple and predictable, so that your focus can be on helping individual readers, writers, and language learners. Within its natural structure, the workshop allows students access to grade-level curriculum through the minilesson and to individualized instruction during the work time, especially through conferences and small-group work.

There is an expectation that every day, all children pursue work that is suited to them as individuals. The classroom is organized and led so that it becomes a supportive, affirmative community, with children working in reciprocal relationships with each other throughout the day to teach and learn from each other. Your role, as the teacher, is to create a respectful, caring community and to channel children to work with engagement on their own important writing and reading projects, talking with each other and with you constantly. And your role is to listen, to adapt, to teach responsively. The simplicity and clarity of the workshop structures allow both your writing and reading workshops to be built around a reverence for listening and for responsive teaching.

> *The simplicity and clarity of the workshop structure allow both your writing and reading workshops to be built around a reverence for listening and for responsive teaching.*

Supplies, Processes, and Schedules

For your MLLs, it is enormously helpful that your writing workshop is as predictable and consistent as possible. It is always important for you to do everything you can to reduce fear and anxiety so that children can learn. A child who is new to learning English can feel panicked when it isn't clear where to secure materials or when or how to do one thing or another. So it is very useful that both the writing and the reading workshops always begin with a minilesson, and children always are asked to bring their materials to the meeting area and to sit in the same spot, on top of their materials. Then, after the minilesson, children know they will always have time to write or read independently while you confer and pull small groups. When work time ends, children know to either meet with partners or gather in the meeting area for a share. The predictability that results from following workshop routines consistently, day after day, provides confidence and a sense of control to multilingual language learners because it allows them to anticipate what will happen next. This decreases their cognitive load and their anxiety, and allows them to focus on their writing (or their reading). The benefits are amplified when workshop structures repeat themselves across other subjects.

Special Considerations for Students in the Early Stages of Language Acquisition

Children who are in the early stages of learning English may often be listening carefully, trying to interpret what is going on around them. It is okay for them to be quiet at this stage; they are taking in a lot of information. However, this listening phase will be short-lived if you provide safe supportive opportunities for English learners to talk and it is critical for you to do so. The English words, phrases, and sentences that will make sense to children in the early stages of English acquisition will probably be predictable sentences related to concrete classroom activities, accompanied by gestures: "Turn and talk," "Bring your folder," and "You can go to your seat now" or "Let's gather in the meeting area."

It is crucial that these learners join the class as best they can from the start. There should never be a time when students at the earliest stages of learning English sit at the edge of the community. If you have new arrivals who are in the silent stage of language acquisition, you may want to organize your class so that some children are in triads instead of in pairs. This can allow for conversation to occur between the two proficient English speakers while the third child is invited to listen, joining in when ready to do so. When organizing these triads, make an effort to group students so that at least one child in a triad will share one of the new arrival's languages, while also being more proficient in English. Pairing students in a variety of ways across the day will also help. Children benefit from same-language partners and from triads and also from being partnered with peers who can function as strong English-language models.

To make these triads and partnerships more powerful, we recommend that you teach everyone in the class to habitually use all forms of communication—gestures, translanguaging, visual props, picture dictionaries, clear examples, and more—and to communicate with one another with patience, humor, and acute, respectful listening.

You may also want to invite English-proficient children to take on the role of a language partner. These children can become a new friend and advocate. We recommend teaching the language partner to first learn all they can from the newcomer. What does the child love to do? What is the child's family like? What language(s) does the child speak? What words can the newcomer teach the proficient English speaker?

The language partner can then have the job of finding five things to teach that can help the youngster join into a writing workshop and five things to help that child join into a reading workshop. Be sure the language partner plays a big role at lunch and recess!

Consistent Teaching Language

Repeat important phrases.

The predictable routines and activities of the workshop provide a comforting structure for students who are acquiring English. It is helpful to use predictable language to indicate the flow of your instruction. If you usually convene your class by saying, "Writers, bring your writing folder, and let's gather," then children who are new to English can still pick up enough to be able to carry on as members of the community.

Even children who are at the earliest stages of learning English can come to understand the predictable phrases that accompany concrete actions. As they come to understand the familiar phrases—"Let's gather," "Bring your folder," "Turn and talk," "Can I have your attention?," and "Off you go"—they develop a sense of belonging in the world of school.

When your reading and writing workshops are characterized by consistent language, this consistent language scaffolds each child's classroom experience. For example, during rehearsal, students will often be invited to "tell your story across your fingers" or to "teach your book, touching each page as you do so." Every time students rehearse their writing, you'll return to this language, building consistency across your instruction. It's helpful if all the adults a child interacts with use the same terminology. For example, if you use the phrase "touch and tell, sketch and write" to guide students' rehearsal, you'll want to encourage all adults who work with your students to use this language as well.

If most of your minilessons begin with you reviewing the content of previous minilessons, perhaps referencing a bullet on a chart, it's helpful for your language learners to know that and for you to use consistent language, such as "Yesterday, we learned . . . ," to clarify when it's the review part of the minilesson. It's also helpful if you start each teaching point by saying, "Today I want to teach you that . . . ," and it's helpful if you repeat your teaching point often and post it on a chart.

Resist overexplaining.

One helpful tip to keep in mind is this: be on guard against the temptation to overtalk during your minilessons. My colleagues and I have sometimes noticed teachers—out of a well-intended effort to communicate clearly—elongating minilessons (and indeed, all teaching) by adding long explanations for words and concepts that might be unfamiliar to some students and by checking on comprehension through constant question-and-answer interruptions. This can lead to minilessons that stretch well past ten minutes and that become convoluted, full of digressions. Avoid this at all costs. The admonition to limit your minilessons to ten minutes is far more important, not less, if your class contains many learners of English.

There may be times when you use guidance from the "Ensuring Access" section to determine what is and is not essential in the minilesson, allowing you to pass lightly over aspects that are not essential—but mostly, you can trust that you'll teach important concepts repeatedly and you can use small-group time, peer support, and the illustrated teaching point to help clarify your teaching, when that's needed.

Choose your own predictable and consistent patterns and phrases.

You'll invent other predictable ways of using consistent language to support your language learners. For example, when you read aloud a mentor text, you may often want to support kids in understanding substitutions, such as when a person is referred to by pronoun rather than name. Those might be instances when you invite kids to do an all-call response. After reading, "He walked down the hall, came and sat with me, and smiled," you might ask, "Who's he?" and use a "come on" gesture to signal you want an all-call response. Then the children can chime in, clarifying the pronoun reference. If the text has talked about a dead whale and referred to that whale as a feast for fish, when the text says, "They swam closer to the feast," you might ask, "What's the feast?" inviting kids to chime in that this is the dead whale. The all-call structure can be supportive for children who feel comfortable joining into a chorus of voices but might not yet feel safe when put on the spot to talk alone.

There are ways to frame questions that make it easier for children to contribute to the discussion. It will be easier for the child to participate if, instead of you asking a question such as, "What is the character feeling?" you frame this by saying, "Looking at her face, I'm thinking she is feeling . . . what? She feels . . . ?" That is, start your thought, then pass the baton, leaving a blank space in the sentence for the child to join in. Of course, this is one of those scaffolds that you will eventually remove.

Consistent Visuals and Gestures

One-Day Charts, Anchor Charts, and Created Charts

The K–2 Units of Study make regular use of visuals, especially through anchor charts and one-day charts. In this way, the units help you provide comprehensible language input for your multilingual language learners. You'll see that the units are filled with charts with headings that clearly state what the chart is about as well as visuals that help children understand key terms that might otherwise feel abstract.

To make these charts even higher leverage, you'll build them together with your students, post them in a central and consistent location in your classroom, and add your own illustrations and examples, drawing on your children's work. It is helpful to reference them often as you teach the whole class and one-on-one.

You'll probably want to give some children individual copies of particular charts. Be sure that you don't overwhelm them with too many personalized charts: be selective and give different charts to different children. To select charts that will be particularly helpful to specific learners, remember that you can draw from charts that support instruction in earlier grade levels. You'll find the most helpful of those charts in *Supporting All Writers: High-Leverage Small Groups and Conferences*, K–2. These charts will allow all your students, and especially your multilingual language learners, to work with more independence since they'll have a visual reference of what they're working on as writers.

Consistent Gestures to Support Comprehensible Teaching

In addition, you'll regularly see suggestions in italics for consistent, predictable gestures that can help you communicate key concepts. For instance, if you're teaching students to stretch out a part of their writing, you might imagine you were holding a rubber band between your hands and dramatically stretch it apart, showing kids how it gets bigger and bigger. When you want kids to think to themselves for a moment, you might tap your head to signal that. Used consistently, and alongside other cues, such as facial expressions and intonation, these gestures will make your teaching more comprehensible and memorable.

Supportive Partnerships

The Benefits of Long-Term Partners

The most important structure that you'll provide to your multilingual language learners will be partnerships. In both your writing and your reading workshops, children will work with a long-term partner. They'll have ample opportunities to talk with partners in a low-stress, highly supportive way. If these children can also speak the same languages, that will provide additional support as they translanguage, work to comprehend both the instruction and the text, and rehearse what they'll write. You'll also channel children to sit beside a partner during the minilesson. Often the minilesson partners and the writing partners are the same, and there are advantages to that.

Strategic Partner Assignments

Pairing a language learner with a child who is stronger in English and also skilled at being a supportive friend is advantageous. Across your class, you might assign all of the partners who are more English proficient to be Partner 1 and all who are English learners to be Partner 2; then, during any one turn-and-talk activity, you can decide whether it is beneficial for the more-proficient English speaker to go first, providing a model, or to go second, allowing the English learner to reach for the most readily available examples. That is, across your day, there are reasons to provide different partnerships to accomplish different jobs.

It is very helpful to show your proficient English speakers ways they can be good partners for English learners. You'll want to emphasize that they need to use everything possible to communicate—gestures, drama, pointing—so that their English-learner friend can understand. Encourage them to then invite their partner to respond, waiting and nodding and gesturing to encourage response. Suggest that they help their partner to recast, saying back what he heard, correcting and adding to it a bit, and then helping him say yet more.

Supporting Students' Language Development

Discussing the Linguistics of Sentences

Navigating Linguistic Challenges with Gestures and Substitutions

There are lots of important ideas that can help you support your English learners' language development. First, you need to become comfortable talking not only about the content of a sentence but also about the linguistics of the sentence, and you need to invite kids to do that as well. A group of staff developers recently examined a passage from *When Lunch Fights Back* by Rebecca L. Johnson:

This is a guide we've given to many English-proficient partners to help them learn to be more helpful to their friends who are learning English.

> A hagfish slithers along the ocean bottom moving like a snake. This primitive deep-sea creature is nearly blind but has a keen sense of smell. It picked up the scent of a dead whale from more than 1 mile away.
>
> The hagfish follows the smell through the water. When it reaches the whale's carcass, it swims towards the remains, sizing up the feast.

The important thing is that you need to see the linguistic challenges in a passage and to be able to observe how your multilingual language learners navigate those challenges. We talked about the nouns in the passage—concrete nouns, such as *hagfish*, can be easier to teach through visuals than verbs. We used gestures to explain the verbs, noting the simile in the first sentence. We acted out the passage, one of us playing the hagfish, one the dead whale. We noted how often the author used substitutions. The hagfish is referred to as "the primitive deep-sea creature" in one place and as "it" in other places. The "dead whale," "the whale's carcass," and the "feast" refer to the same thing. This work draws on the research of Hasan and Halliday, who are known for their groundbreaking work on text cohesion.

What to Leave Out—and What to Put into Writing

In *Cohesion in English* (1976), Halliday and Hasan discuss the importance of understanding what makes a text a cohesive unit. They outline five types of cohesion within and among sentences. For instance, sentences might include references, where one sentence uses nouns and the next uses pronouns to refer to the same thing (Carla and Jasper ran to the playground. *They* slid down the slide.). Or sentences might include conjunctions, linking successive sentences that are not structurally related with words such as *and, however, as a result,* or *previously*. After students study what other writers leave out of their sentences, they can more easily make decisions about what to leave out of their own writing and require their readers to fill in.

As you pull up next to one of your multilingual language learners and confer, try to perceive the language challenges she encountered in her writing. The writing that some youngsters do will seem oddly repetitive to you, and you may find, upon closer examination, that this is a writer who could benefit from encouragement to use substitutions. Of course, other writers will have used many pronouns and may need to clarify to whom or what each pronoun refers. Since most youngsters find verb tenses challenging, you'll have opportunities to instruct in ways that are immediately relevant to your language learners' writing.

Studying "Juicy" Sentences, Punctuation, and More

Having students study sentences closely will support them as they work to write more complex sentences. Lily Wong Fillmore suggests that you gather small groups of students to talk over the meaning of "juicy sentences," as she refers to a passage that she asks children to examine closely. Others refer to the same work as "a language dive." The children first read the passage on their own and summarize it as best they can, then the group discusses the passage, chunk by chunk. You take a back seat when doing this work, mostly asking questions and engaging kids in doing

> *As you pull up next to one of your multilingual language learners and confer, try to perceive the language challenges she encountered in her writing.*

the work of figuring out the passage. Ask, "What other word could the author have used here?" or "Could this phrase/word be removed without changing the meaning of this sentence?" and even "Could this sentence go in a different order—moving chunks of it around—and mean the same thing?"

There are, of course, many ways to set students up to think and talk about how language works. They might look at how question marks are used in English and in Spanish, deepening their understanding of both languages as they study differences in punctuation. You might invite your multilingual language learners to share the words they know for an important word—say, *opinion*—in all the languages they speak. Ask them to compare a text, written in two languages they can read and write, and to talk about the language choices used. Ask them to say or write in any language that the students know well other than English and then translate that passage (use a translation website or application if that helps) into English. Then suggest that the students compare the two versions. Or ask a few children to spend some time noticing the similarities and differences between the language used in a story and the language used in a science expository text. The children won't name a particular change in a part of speech, as when a verb such as *float* is made into a noun, *flotation,* nor will they name dense noun groups such as "the soccer-ball sized head"—but they will benefit from you asking, "Is the subject here soccer or is it head?"

Supporting Vocabulary Building and Knowledge of Academic English

One of your major goals across writing workshop will be to help students build their vocabularies and to use the new words they are learning as they talk and write.

Support students in building vocabulary using their own writing as the context.

Multilingual language learners benefit not only from explicit vocabulary instruction but also from opportunities to use new vocabulary. This means that one way to make vocabulary instruction especially powerful is to center it around students' own writing. If students are writing about a particular nonfiction topic, you might gather those students together and collaboratively build a bank of vocabulary words they could use with writing, acting out some of the words or using images to make the new vocabulary clear for students. If the students in a group are writing about weather, for instance, you might introduce a bank of related vocabulary: *clouds, cloudy, rainy, sunny, thermometer, storm, extreme, meteorologist, report.* Then, you could coach students to use this bank of words as they rehearse and draft.

You may be thinking, "In the Units of Study curriculum, students don't generally write about shared topics," and that is true. But remember that both the child who is writing about breaking an arm and the one writing about getting a mysterious rash are writing about medical crises, and both might be able to draw on a word bank that includes *injury, appointment, examine,* and *medicine.*

You'll adjust your vocabulary support based on your learners' knowledge of English. For students at the earliest stages of language acquisition, especially those who are drawing representationally but not yet putting many words down on the page, you might provide help with labeling what they have drawn. "Is this the swing?" you might ask, touching a drawing of a swing. "Say *swing.* Is this the sky? Are these your friends?" You might also help the child talk about the drawing in sentences, perhaps using one sentence stem repeatedly: "This is the swing. This is the sky. The sky is . . . blue. Is it sunny or cloudy? Yes, the sky is sunny." This is a supportive way to introduce many Tier 1 vocabulary words that your multilingual language learners will probably know in other languages but may not yet know in English.

Scaffold students' work in writing with description and specificity.

It is helpful to support multilingual language learners in the use of more descriptive and extended language. Although your whole-class teaching across any unit will support this goal, it will also be important to devote small-group and one-on-one time to this important endeavor.

If a child overuses a word such as *nice* or *beautiful*, you will want to help the youngster learn that there are many different, more precise words that she could use. You might ask, "Is the person lovely? Impressive? Unusual? Dignified? Cute?" Some teachers help children to develop word files, with the overused word at the center of a card and five variations of that word around the edges. Then children can keep these cards on hand throughout the day and look for opportunities to use specific words orally.

Within the *Supporting All Writers: High-Leverage Small Groups and Conferences, K–2*, book, you'll find several progressions of small groups and conferences designed to help kids say more and to add onto their writing with precise, strategically chosen language. For instance, you might teach students to add to their writing *what* happened, and *when*, *where*, and *how* it happened. Or you might teach students how to write with comparisons, using phrases such as *fast as a train* or *she is fancy like a rose*. Oral rehearsal is key here—you want to give children the chance to elaborate through talk before they put the words down on paper. Lean on published mentor texts, kid-written mentor texts that are authored by classmates, and your own demonstration writing to help illustrate these concepts.

When analyzing a student's writing for language goals, it can be easy to fixate on what the student is not doing, noticing issues in word order, tense, subject-verb agreement, use of transition words, and inaccurate pronoun references, among others. We recommend that you rely on the advice of What Works Clearinghouse (2014) and look instead for just one or two aspects of writing that will make the biggest difference to your multilingual language learners. Then you can provide some explicit instruction in those especially high-leverage areas.

While concrete nouns and high-utility verbs are generally easier for learners to pick up, you also want to support multilingual language learners in acquiring the critical connector words and transitions that support more complex sentence structures. That is, once students begin using the higher-frequency transitions, such as *and, but, because*, and *then*, you can expand that repertoire to include more sophisticated transitions, such as *even though*. To help students learn to write using complex sentences, scaffold them to speak using those sentences. One important way to do so is to help them talk with more proficient English speakers as they engage in activities that involve cause-and-effect work. If children are figuring out how to build a working volcano, they'll probably use transition words such as *because* and *however*. Hiebert (2013) points out that "the vocabulary of complex concepts cannot be gained simply from definitions in glossaries. Because the words of information texts are interrelated, teachers provide students with in-depth experiences that allow for concept development. Such experiences are frequently hands-on and involve follow-up discussions, such as an experiment to demonstrate gravity, building a model of a triangle and labeling the hypotenuse, making a diagram of photosynthesis with arrows and descriptions, or making a map with the lines of longitude. A multisensory experience is best so that students can experience the concept, discuss it, record it, write it, and apply it (Cervetti, Pearson, Bravo, & Barber, 2006)."

Teaching Figurative Language

Children learning English will also need support as they come to understand and use figurative language. Literature is filled with metaphors, similes, and idioms, as are the minilessons in this series. Children who are just on the brink of learning academic English will profit from some small-group instruction that gives them access to literary devices. Again, shared writing can be a wonderful method to support students in studying, reading, and discussing figurative language. Word sorts where students read an idiom or phrase and determine whether it is positive or negative can give students exposure to new language in a fun way. You might even decide to introduce students to a new phrase each week, challenging them to use that phrase whenever they can across the week and then to add it to their bank of figurative language.

Grammar and Parts of Speech

You'll find that we have included some very accessible instruction in grammar and parts of speech in the second-grade curriculum. We suggest that you provide this instruction outside the reading and writing workshops. We refer to this teaching as "extensions" and suggest that you tuck this instruction into small intervals of your school day: the moments when kids have packed up their backpacks and are waiting for the bus, the few minutes of wait time before a special. The grammar instruction is fast-paced, interactive, and mostly oral. Kids work with partners to point to five concrete nouns, to take sentence fragments and rewrite them as full sentences, to do a quick hunt through their books for sentences that are punctuated with something other than a period. One day's teaching builds on the next—so the kids are taught that every sentence has a noun, and then that instruction is revised as they learn about pronouns. Always, the instruction is brought home to their writing, for example: "With your partner, look back at the first page of what you wrote today and check to see if, in fact, each of your sentences has a noun and a verb."

There is a sequence to this grammar instruction, moving from less complex to more complex across a unit, and across the year. In the first unit with grammar extensions, you'll address capitalization and punctuation in Bend I; word types, such as nouns and verbs, in Bend II; and past, present, and future tenses in Bend III. In the subsequent units that have grammar extensions, you'll begin with sessions about sentences and word types (adjectives, adverbs, nouns, and verbs). Later, you'll transition to sessions that address more subtle areas of grammar, such as conjunctions, prepositions, and apostrophes. Then, you'll focus on whole-sentence work, such as expanding simple sentences and forming complex sentences.

Your children will not master grammar because of this instruction, but they will become aware of a metalinguistic way to talk and think about language. They'll also become acquainted with grammar terminology, so you can talk about grammar when responding to their writing. If a child uses a noun over and over and you want to suggest he use synonyms or pronoun substitutions, you and the youngster will have a vocabulary that makes that conversation easier . . . and that helps the child be more deliberate in his sentence construction.

Co-planning with a Language Specialist to Maximize Learning in the Writing Workshop

If classroom teachers and language specialists have opportunities to plan together, the language specialist can support the children during the workshop. The language specialist might:

- **Preteach the concepts and vocabulary necessary for understanding the big teaching points.** We have videoed previews for each lesson, but a specialist who knows the youngsters involved can tailor these to those children. If the minilesson teaches children how to write using main ideas and supporting ideas, the language specialist might use a nonfiction content-area book and lots of gestures to convey that the title of each chapter shows the main idea and that some of the subtitles are supporting ideas (or smaller ideas). The phrase *learn the lingo* is used to refer to learning new vocabulary words—the language specialist might give some examples or teach what the word *lingo* means in this context.

- **Work with students to target specific parts of language.** The language specialist might use shared reading or interactive writing as a way to build language structures. For instance, narratives are usually written in past tense and the specialist might help children learn to vary their verbs based on whether the action is occurring now or occurred in the past.

- **Support phonological awareness—segmenting and hearing sounds in words—as well as learning English phonics—starting with letters and sounds** to represent those sounds with graphemes. In kindergarten, this work is already in the curriculum and all children can do this together. In first and second grade, the language specialist will have to assess to determine what students know and can apply of English phonics to know what to teach, how to coach, and what to set as appropriate expectations and tasks.

- **Provide simple language prompts.** Prioritize prompts that the writer can use again and again so as to teach toward independence. For instance, when reading for information, the writer might benefit from prompts such as "I notice . . ." and "I wonder . . ."

Establishing a Classroom Culture that Celebrates All the Languages Your Students Speak

Especially for our youngest learners, it's important to foster awareness around how different languages sound and look. Look for opportunities to celebrate and include all the languages your students speak. You might invite families into the classroom to share the different languages they speak. You might talk about the different ways stories end in different languages. Even posting a welcome sign in all the languages your children speak sends an important message.

In every unit, provide or create resources across your classroom in multiple languages—books, checklists, charts, signs, labels, greetings, students' writing—and honor them all. Do what you can to create signs and labels in as many languages as may be relevant for your class—perhaps even more. Let's work, as a community of educators, to develop and share supports for children who come to us speaking all the languages in the world. Working together, we can help each other locate mentor texts in as many relevant languages as possible. Our children deserve no less.

Ensuring Access

Helping All Learners across the Curriculum

9

Ensuring Access
Helping All Learners across the Curriculum

T he aim of this chapter is to address the challenges and promises of ensuring that writing instruction is accessible to all your children, especially your students for whom learning to write is particularly fraught with obstacles. Surely, there are few topics that matter more.

As I discussed in Chapter 8, because the structure of the writing workshop and its sister, the reading workshop, is deliberately kept simple and predictable, the workshop allows you to focus on helping individual writers and readers. This means that while your minilessons allow your children to access grade-level curriculum, you can individualize your instruction through conferences and small-group work.

Within this chapter, I will discuss ways in which you can support a range of learners, and particularly those who would benefit from additional or specific support in writing. This includes but is not limited to students with disabilities that affect writing and students for whom their expected trajectory of writing development is simply not going as hoped. Since writing is a high-leverage skill that has echoing effects across the curriculum, it is particularly important to ensure that students' writing skills are the strongest they can be. I hope that this chapter gives you not only practical strategies for ensuring access but also renewed energy for this rewarding work.

Take the time you need to truly assess.

Sometimes when working with children who have particular needs in writing, we are so determined to *do something* that we react with understandable urgency before we really understand who the child is and what the child needs. The visibility of writing—the fact that we can see exactly what a child can do or is not yet doing—can intensify the desire to take quick action. That feeling of wanting to urgently solve the problem and to do so right away, with a solution that can be put in place immediately, often leads to remedies that promise to be a solve-all solution, but that actually do too little.

How important it is to be wary. One thing that is an absolute truth about kids who have trouble writing is this: there neither is nor will ever be a one-size-fits-all approach that will meet every need. And it is a real problem when we subject a child who especially needs to be seen, understood, and supported to one more battery of fill-in-the-blank worksheets, one more computer program, and one more after-school intervention, all of which miss the mark. Too many children have languished for too long in failed fix-all interventions, receiving instruction that most certainly does not meet their very real and pressing needs. To address this issue, you need to engage in assessment as a way not only to identify *who* needs help, but also to guide you in figuring out *what* help is needed and *how* to provide that help.

Starting the Year with Baseline Assessments

The start of the school year is a critical time for meaningful assessment. Your students' previous year's teachers will hopefully have passed along data about children's writing performances, allowing your assessments to be more efficient. You will also have started by administering your school's universal reading screener—which, while usually not explicitly focused on writing, can give you some insights into possible underlying issues that need to be addressed also in writing. Take those screeners into account as you formulate your plan for supporting your writers.

In *Writing Pathways, K–2*, which is included in your resources, you'll find assessments, checklists, exemplar texts, annotated benchmark pieces of writing, and more, at each level for all three genres. These can help you assess. Kids will also assess their own work using familiar anchor charts. Be sure that if your district requires you to use an assessment tool, such as a district- or statewide beginning-of-the-year or interim writing prompt, you don't duplicate assessments by using a tool we suggest if it is redundant. Nothing is more important than using your time with your students in meaningful ways, so if information can be pulled from other sources, even if you believe those tools are less than ideal, we encourage you to reduce needless assessments.

As you get to know your students, you'll construct a portrait of each writer in your class. This may be an actual document, or it may just be your internalized sense of each writer, but either way, it is important. Your understanding of each of your writers will be based on a letter-sound or spelling assessment, on your phonic decoding assessments, on any on-demand writing pieces, and on writing samples taken from the student's work across the school day. Your portrait of each writer will also draw on your observations during writing workshops and your personal connection with the child. It is

hard to emphasize enough how important it is for you to take time during your writing workshop to simply scan your room, noting your writers' behaviors. You can draw on this data as you design your instruction.

Writing Behaviors to Look Out For

It is worth mentioning that, although there is a lot of reciprocity in reading and writing, there are a handful of things specific to writing that you will want to be on the lookout for as you watch your students during those first weeks of school. While some of these items only affect writing, most also give a window into a child's reading. Many of these behaviors will be touched upon throughout this chapter.

- **Pencil/pen grip:** Occupational therapists tell us that pencil grip is still fluid and developing until halfway through second grade. If you notice that your students in late kindergarten through mid-second grade have not yet developed proficiency with the tripod grip, you might want to offer additional coaching or seek advice from your school's occupational therapist.

- **Efficient and automatic letter formation:** There will come a time when, after explicit instruction on letter formation, you will want to keep an eye out for children who clearly need extra support with this. Check whether the challenge comes from the child needing support with letter-sound connection or whether it's fine-motor skills that are needed.

- **Additional letters in words:** If you see a student adding additional consonants into words—and these are not consonants that are connected to the sounds one might hear when a word is stretched—you might want to follow up with a letter-sound assessment to see whether there is a pattern you can address. Also watch the child in the act of spelling a word. He might be saying the word once and recording sounds he hears, then saying the whole word again and again, recording yet more salient sounds each time. Take note if the writer adds a *U* or an *A* after a voiced consonant, such as *B*, *D*, or *K*. For example, if the child's spelling of *sad* ends with a *U* or an *A*, chances are that child is sounding out the /d/ as if its sound is *duh* and adding the letters to capture that sound.

- **Missing letters in words:** You can expect that in kindergarten, children will hear only the most salient sounds in a word, but by late kindergarten, you'll expect children to hear some of the more subtle sounds. Take note when a child does not represent most of the sounds in words. That might be a clue that the child needs more support with phonological awareness. Do some further investigation.

- **Avoidance behaviors:** It helps to remember the adage: behavior is communication. Notice if a child continually needs to visit the restroom or get a drink of water during workshop time. Notice if a child is regularly consumed with illustrations and conversations and gets no writing done. Consider whether there is some avoidance at play. If you compliment the child, do those avoidance behaviors decrease?

While observations like these can't give you all the information you need to formulate a plan, they can give you valuable insights that can lead to more investigation that will help you get the answers you need.

What does it mean to individualize writing instruction based on assessment?

Although workshops are designed to be absolutely responsive, there isn't one among us who doesn't need to do more to be sure that our teaching truly helps all our learners. It's helpful to know clues that can signal that a writing workshop may not be as supportive of all kids as it needs to be.

Of course, thinking about making a writing workshop more accessible and more responsive requires time and attention. If you decide to prioritize this work—and I'd argue that this merits becoming a priority for you—then you will want to clear out time and space in your teaching for it. You cannot be all things as a teacher; you cannot prioritize everything. And there won't be time in your writing workshop for everything to be equally important.

Consider which aspects of your teaching currently require your time and attention and weigh whether you approve of your own priorities. Are you spending inordinate amounts of time ensuring that your children's publications are really special? Are you especially invested in record keeping—and yet notice that you don't actually use those records much? Are there ways to outsource some of what is consuming your time or your children's time? Might a few parent volunteers help with publication? Might you make your author celebrations vastly simpler? Might you get an app that helps you streamline your record keeping?

Doug Reeves (2013) suggests that before any educator can do something more, it is necessary to pull the weeds to make space for new stuff to grow. And Warren Buffett, one of the world's top investors, said, "People ask me for the secret of my success. It's my ability to say *no*. Day in and day out, I look at investment proposals and I say, 'No, no, no, no.' Then one comes along that looks exactly right and I say yes. One *yes* can get you very far." You and I are, in a sense, investors. We look over proposals for what will help our students, and we, like Warren Buffett, need to say, "No, no, no, no." Then when one comes along that looks exactly right, we can say *yes*. And one yes can take us very far. It's important that we take the time and have the courage to be self-critical and to question some of what we are doing now. To do more to grant all kids access to the richest possible writing instruction, we need to be willing to say no to some things that are taking up our time, our children's time, and that may not be helping us be the educator we want to be.

Taking Stock of Your Teaching

Here are some ways to reflect on how responsive and accessible your teaching is:

- Consider, for a moment, the children who concern you most. Bring one of those children to mind. What talent does this kid have? What is the child's genius? What have you done to make sure the child sees that you recognize this genius? What have you done to be sure *all* your kids recognize this child's genius? It would not be easy for any one of us to do good work if the people around us didn't value our gifts enough to expect good work from us.

- Think about how your kids are doing as writers. Form an opinion before reading on. If just now, you thought of your class as mostly a monolith, thinking something like, "My kids are really behind," or "My kids are precocious," this should be a wake-up call to you. Kids are different, and you are probably glossing over those differences. Your class will always contain a wide and wonderful variety of strengths and needs.

- If your kids spend a good portion of their time all writing about the same sorts of things, and if they work at roughly the same level, using the same sorts of strategies, you'll want to focus on discerning the level of challenge each of your kids can handle and providing each child with the invitations and supports that child needs.

- If your kids' seating arrangement, or really, their anything, is basically all the same, then you haven't yet figured out optimal ways to support each idiosyncratic learner. Might some kids benefit from sitting on the floor during writing time? Might some benefit from writing with headphones (allowing for silence or for music)? Might some benefit from writing standing up, using a standing desk, tall shelf, or even a wall to lean against? Might one partnership of kids benefit from coauthoring?

- If your children are mostly holding the same charts, writing utensils, paper, or other tools, then you haven't yet helped each child figure out what he or she needs—and does not need—in the way of tools and scaffolds. If your kids are mostly writing with the same tool, in the same way, you haven't yet helped them figure out their individual learning needs and preferences.

- Think about the reason why some of your kids are not yet writing at benchmark. Answer the question "Why?" before you read on. If your answer was that they don't have anything to write about, they can't sustain engagement for long, or they don't spell words conventionally, then you haven't yet embraced the complex ways in which kids are different as writers.

- To add on, if your answer to the question asking why some kids are not yet writing at grade benchmark levels was all about them and not about any of *your* actions, you aren't yet taking responsibility. If your answer was essentially a way of saying "She isn't . . ." or "He hasn't . . . ," start rephrasing that to say, "She probably would benefit from . . ." or "He needs more support and instruction in . . ." or "I need to do better at. . . ."

- If all the classrooms across your grade level have almost exactly the same tools, you and your colleagues probably haven't yet devised solutions in response to idiosyncratic needs and opportunities that your particular community of children will need this year.

The Units of Study are strength based.

It is easy when one starts with assessment to be drawn quickly to all of what is *not* there, what is missing and needs to be added. I understand that instinct. After all, so many assessments are designed to show areas where a student will need additional assistance—and now, more than ever, those needs feel urgent. However, kids aren't that different from you and me. Like us, they will thrive when their strengths are recognized,

not just their weaknesses. Children delight in hearing about what you admire about them and in being complimented for the things they are good at and are working hard on. Because of this, you will find that the teaching in each unit is staunchly on the side of marveling over and building upon the strengths of your students.

This is true for all students, of course. But it is especially true for students for whom school has not always been a bed of roses. With so many well-intentioned initiatives, interventions, and supports, it is not unusual for students to be labeled early and often by what they *cannot* do rather than by what they *can* do. For students to receive Tier 3 level services or an Individualized Education Program (IEP), they must be deemed to have weaknesses in comparison with their peers. The unfortunate reality is that to receive what a child most needs, she must be subjected to a series of experiences meant to tease out and spotlight what she cannot do. Those *cannots* quickly become the student's identity. Your students go from being Lana, Diego, and Miles to "writing kid," "IEP kid," and "struggling writer." And, whether or not anyone calls our students by those labels to their faces, those labels affect the way you and others interact with your students. A focus on students' weaknesses reduces the opportunity for building upon a sturdy foundation of strength.

> *Kids aren't that different from you and me. Like us, they will thrive when their strengths are recognized, not just their weaknesses.*

Every student, every learning profile, comes with a package of strengths and needs. The child who benefits from revisiting a writing strategy and doing so in many many different modalities is also the child who knocks your socks off with a beautifully poetic ending to a story. The child who needs support when interacting socially is also the child who uses rich material, packed with facts, for information writing. It may at first sound like a warm fuzzy platitude for me to say, "The Units of Study are strength-based" but this declaration stands on the shoulders of decades of educational scholarship by the likes of Dewey, Vygotsky, Ladson-Billings, Gonzalez, and Morrell. It's especially important to value students' strengths and center their identities in a writing workshop because the entire curriculum is intimately connected to their lives.

Of course, there are times and ways in which your goal will be to teach into a child's needs. In those instances, you will be most successful when you begin with what you know about the child's strengths. This, of course, assumes that you have studied and recorded strengths as part of your initial assessment of your students. If you have not yet done that work, it is critical and widely valuable work to do today. By building upon a student's strengths, not only do you ensure that you are teaching within the child's zone of proximal development, you also ensure that the child is set up for success.

Examples of Leveraging Students' Strengths to Teach into Their Needs

If a student has this strength . . .	And also this need . . .	You might . . .
This writer is a "natural" verbal storyteller. He comes to school every morning with tales of his adventures and often has you and his classmates hanging on to his every word.	The learner needs explicit, sequential instruction in phonics to develop proficiency in encoding. He sometimes avoids writing or writes very little, and his writing is not very readable.	• Determine which phonics concepts have already been taught so that you may refer to relevant mnemonics and other tools when coaching into the student's writing. • Make sure that the child has ready access to any tools or charts being used in phonics instruction so that he can use them as references when aiming to record his thoughts during workshop time. • Offer the child access to a recording device or an app that allows him to record his voice so as to not lose his ideas while trying to record them. It will also allow him to hear the same sentence and phrase over and over again to isolate and record the sounds.
This is a flexible and spontaneous student who thrives on movement and socializing. She has a lot to say, and she initiates a lot of ideas. Other children listen to her.	This writer needs support to work independently for a length of time without becoming distracted. She often needs guidance in pacing and task completion.	• Create a writing agenda, in consultation with the writer, that breaks down writing workshop time into smaller, more manageable chunks. If possible, number these steps and include visuals so that she can keep track of progress. • If you have a number of children with this pattern, create a movement break prior to writing or schedule writing time after physical education class, allowing the children to release some of their energy in ways that make focusing a bit easier. • Encourage this child to rehearse for writing by pacing and talking, saying her story in a whisper as she walks up and down the hall or paces back and forth across an area of your classroom. • Provide a visual timer and agenda so that the child can take frequent, but timed, movement breaks. During those breaks, encourage her to mentally or verbally rehearse what she will write when break time is over.
This is the class professor—filled with information about topics of interest. He shares that information with any and all who will listen.	The writer needs support with story elements, especially character feelings and story plots. Even when the unit is narrative, this writer tends to lean toward writing information texts.	• Create a box or folder where the student can collect sketches, photographs, or objects connected to a topic of interest. When narrative writing comes, ask the student to choose one item to build a story off of—using the class or demonstration story as a mentor. • Explicitly teach the language and syntax of story. Using sketches of faces that show emotions, teach the student a range of language to describe emotion. Use sentence frames to cue and perhaps serve as a scaffold for drafting different parts of a story: "One day I . . .", "Suddenly I . . .," "I was so . . . ! I said, ..." • Ask your student to choose a favorite narrative mentor text—ideally, one that is simple and accessible. When your student rehearses and then later drafts, encourage him to refer frequently to the mentor author, especially when it comes to story structure and emotion. You might say, "Oh look! Here the author shows us how there's trouble in the story. What trouble will be in your story?" Meanwhile, spotlight the writer during your information units.

Writing Workshop and MTSS/RTI

Since 1975, when the Individuals with Disabilities Education Act (IDEA) came into being in its earliest iteration, it has not only been ethical, moral, and humane to go to great lengths to support all learners, it has also been the law. Over the years, the ways this law has been enacted both legally and practically have evolved. As of the writing of this book, the most recent evolution involves the Every Student Succeeds Act (ESSA).

What are Multi-Tiered Systems of Support and Response to Intervention?

A Multi-Tiered System of Support (MTSS), which is outlined within ESSA, is a comprehensive and systematic framework that provides academic and behavioral supports for all students based on their individual needs. It looks at three aspects that can have a direct impact on students' school performance: academic, social and emotional learning, and behavioral learning. It aims to guide schools and districts to think about the systems of support for individual success, considering a variety of aspects such as resources, professional development, and leadership.

Response to Intervention (RTI) falls under the umbrella framework of MTSS and is specifically focused on academic needs. RTI is also a multitiered approach, and it begins in the classroom with the implementation of a high-quality core curriculum, as well as universal screening and ongoing progress monitoring of all students. As the school year and curriculum progress, if students are not making adequate progress, the level of support can escalate through the various tiers. RTI is used when making decisions regarding both general education and special education since continual progress monitoring allows for assessment of how individual students are responding to varied levels and intensity of interventions. It is important to note that the family can request an evaluation for the child at any time, regardless of whether or not the child has moved through all of the RTI tiers.

Most students are provided with Tier 2 and Tier 3 interventions because of reading and/or math needs. However, writing is one of the core academic subjects and eligible for intervention when appropriate. Additionally, the link between writing and reading growth is strong. In the primary grades, when so much of decoding and comprehension reinforcement occurs during writing workshop, intervention in writing can pay large dividends not only in writing growth but, thrillingly, in exponential reading growth as well.

Three Tiers of Supportive Instruction

Both MTSS and RTI require that schools provide three tiers of instruction. Tier 1 refers to high-quality, whole-class core instruction. This includes all aspects of whole-class instruction—small-group work, conferring, differentiated materials—everything that you provide in a typical writing workshop. Every child in your class is considered to be in Tier 1. Your goal is to design your instruction in such a way as to remove possible obstacles to learning, creating multiple access points to the grade-level curriculum. If a child receives this strong, well-resourced whole-class instruction and the data shows he is still not making the hoped-for progress, the supports that student receives are escalated to Tier 2.

Tier 2 supports include the continuation of high-quality whole-class instruction, with the addition of more intensive, targeted instruction matched to student needs. This intervention can vary across group size, frequency, and duration, but is often provided in small groups and offered by the teacher or perhaps a specialist. Again, this level of support is in addition to Tier 1 support, not in place of it. If, after a time (which will vary from district to district but is typically eight to twelve weeks), a student is still not making the hoped-for progress, the child is then considered for more intensive, Tier 3 intervention. At Tier 3, the child will of course continue to receive the Tier 1 core curriculum but will also receive individualized, more intensive supports, typically in a one-to-one scenario with a specialist outside of the classroom setting. The students in Tier 3 will continue to be progress monitored, since oftentimes students who do not show the desired level of growth in response to such targeted interventions are then referred for a comprehensive evaluation and considered for eligibility for special education services.

Evaluating Students for Appropriate Levels of Support

Each child that has specific core needs, such as writing, will be discussed by a team that extends beyond you to decide whether the child needs Tier 2 or 3 intervention. "What does the data show us that this child needs? Can it be addressed through further differentiation or adjustments to the Tier 1 curriculum or is she in need of additional support?" A proposal will emerge. For one child, the plan might be: "Perhaps we make modifications to the core curriculum by providing this student with a few tools that will help her during independent writing—one that is a reminder about the spaces between letters and words and one that is a reminder of how each letter is formed. When you are working with the student you can coach into those tools, and then after four weeks you can assess whether or not those tools are still needed." In this case, the child's needs may be appropriately addressed through scaffolds provided in Tier 1.

Another scenario may involve a student who needs more targeted instruction in addition to the Tier 1 curriculum. For this child, the plan might be: "It's already January and while this first-grade writer is a great storyteller, most of her story is told in the pictures and in her accompanying oral rendition. When pushed to write a sentence to accompany her sketches, the words she does write typically have only beginning and ending sounds and contain no vowels. It might be helpful to provide her with some targeted phonics instruction to address these gaps." In this particular case, differentiation of the Tier 1 curriculum would not provide the needed supports, and instead the team would decide to elevate to Tier 2.

These teams generally go with the assumption that approximately 75 or 80% of the general student population will be well served in Tier 1, 20 to 25% will require the additional focus in Tier 2, and a very small percentage will need the most intensive support, Tier 3. As the year progresses, those figures are expected to change a bit because if a child makes no progress in Tier 1, that youngster is shifted to Tier 2, and so it goes. A static placement of students in tiers is something that should signal you to look more closely.

What does a Multi-Tiered System of Support look like in practice?

Tier 1 Instruction

Tier 1, since it is provided by the classroom teacher in the classroom, can look many different ways. Because workshop teaching is responsive, it is quite common to see teachers making modifications and providing scaffolds as student needs arise. Perhaps a few children need to say what they hope to write aloud over and over, tapping and touching each page before they write. Perhaps a few children would benefit from coauthoring their books, working with a teammate to plan and write. Perhaps a few children would benefit from extra support for phonemic awareness and some phonemic-awareness activities or games on a regular basis. Maybe one writer might be working in a triad rather than a partnership.

You'll probably meet with groups of children who need support fairly often. These groups tend to last for at least a week, perhaps meeting on alternating days so that in between those meetings, children have time to practice what has been taught. When progress isn't made with one sort of help, you will use what you have learned to vary that help. That is, high-quality classroom instruction in writing is critical.

While classroom-based interventions are underway, you will regularly monitor student progress toward writing goals and make adjustments to instruction, providing necessary levels of support until all your students are able to show successful growth. However, if all your efforts don't yield, you may decide that a child needs more support, in which case the child shifts to Tier 2. It is important to realize that children shift between Tier 1 and Tier 2 and back to Tier 1 fairly easily, and none of this goes on the learner's lasting record.

Tier 2 Instruction

While specifics vary district to district, state to state, children needing Tier 2 instruction typically receive an extra thirty minutes of support, three days a week, in needs-based groups of three to five students, for eight to twelve weeks. This support can be provided by the classroom teacher but must be in addition to the core Tier 1 curriculum. Alternatively, Tier 2 instruction can be provided by a qualified interventionist who might pull the students out of class or come into the workshop and work with the children in small groups during work time. Again, this support is provided in addition to, not in place of, Tier 1 writing instruction. When scheduling it's important to try not to remove students from reading, writing, or math instruction for intervention.

Tier 3 Instruction

If a child does not make tangible progress even when receiving Tier 2 support, the child moves to Tier 3, where instruction will be intensified. In Tier 3, the child will receive intensive, individualized instruction (in a scientific research-based intervention) from a trained professional. Shifts that commonly occur as a child moves from Tier 2 to 3 include smaller group size, perhaps even one-to-one support, as well as an increase in frequency and/or duration. This support occurs outside of the classroom in addition to the Tier 1 support provided in the general education classroom. This level of support is typically reserved for 1 to 5% of students. For these interventions, teachers and specialists often choose to draw on supplemental programs designed to target students' specific needs.

Reflect: A Quick Check of Your Support Structures

Before leaving this topic, let's pause for a moment to take stock. I hope you have recognized the implications to this chapter. Here are some important bits of cautionary advice.

- If you have more than 20% of your kids receiving Tier 2 services, or more than 5% receiving Tier 3 supports, that suggests you need to examine the levels of support you are providing for kids within your classroom.

- If your kids are placed in Tier 1, 2, or 3 at the start of the year and those assignments never change, this is worrisome, suggesting you may not be collecting and analyzing data often enough.

- If you have students missing core subjects (reading, writing, and math) to receive interventions outside of the classroom, this is problematic. Speak with your administration about the scheduling of these interventions to ensure students are receiving their core instruction.

Adjust the sequence of units based on your data.

Although you will assess all your children and carefully consider ways you can develop a plan for supporting their individual needs, it will also be important to consider ways your whole-class teaching will take into account those needs.

Teaching Units to Bring Up Below-Benchmark Students

There are a few ways you might adjust your sequence of units based on your data. If your assessments reveal that students' skills are currently far below grade-level benchmarks, you might choose to alter your intended sequence of units for the year and borrow a unit

or two from your lower-grade colleagues. For instance, after returning to in-person school during the pandemic, when teachers needed to consider ways to support whole classes of kids whose schooling had been fragmented and chaotic, many first-grade teachers chose to teach *Writing for Readers*—a unit that supports writing readable books and spelling by both sounding out words and drawing on a knowledge of phonics and sight vocabulary. Many second-grade teachers began the school year by teaching *Small Moments*, which is a first-grade unit.

Maintaining Appropriate Pacing

There are, of course, caveats. First, if you begin by teaching a unit from the previous year or take a detour to do so, keep in mind that you will also want to have time to teach the curriculum for your grade level, or at least most of it—so be sure your units are well paced. While it is crucial that your instruction meet kids where they are, kids also must receive their grade-level curriculum or we risk continuing a cascading effect of some children not quite getting all of one grade's riches.

It is also important that the teachers at a grade level form a community of practice, meeting often to plan teaching, sharing insights and tools, and providing help to each other. We do not recommend that you or a colleague go rogue. If you think it is best to teach a unit or two from the preceding grade, convince your colleagues to do likewise. If that is not possible for an entire grade team, partner up with another teacher for the unit in question so that you have a thought partner while detouring. And make sure that after the detour, you get your scope and sequence back in alignment.

> *It is also important that the teachers at a grade level form a community of practice, meeting often to plan teaching, sharing insights and tools, and providing help to each other.*

Taking a Break between Units

Another way to adapt your whole-class curriculum is by occasionally taking a break from units to address some needs. For example, if you are a kindergarten teacher about to teach Unit 3, *Writing for Readers*, you'll want to be sure your youngsters are ready to take advantage of the opportunities the unit provides. If you have children who do not yet have strong sound-letter knowledge, you may decide to teach that phonics curriculum during both phonics and writing for a week or two so that your students bring precursor skills to *Writing for Readers*. To do this, you can draw on the "Cumulative Review of Letter/Sound Knowledge," available in the online resources, and in *Supporting All Writers: High-Leverage Small Groups and Conferences, K–2*. This book contains many small groups that you could teach.

Altering Your Schedule

You might also consider altering your schedule for a month by teaching your writing workshop only three times a week to devote time for centers that support specific needs twice a week. For example, after the pandemic, many teachers found that their kindergarten and first-grade children needed many more opportunities to develop their fine motor control. Some master teachers decided to design learning centers to help with that and to space out Unit 1 so that those centers occurred twice a week in lieu of their reading or writing workshop. One of those centers channeled kids to garden—they were given scissors and instructed to trim back each tiny branch of the hedge outside the classroom in ways that helped their fine motor control. I'm not advocating for gardening but, instead, suggesting that wise classroom teachers study what children need, talk with colleagues about adjustments that they believe will help, and then implement them, recognizing that these are temporary supports. And, ultimately, trimming the hedges (or creating intricately designed scissor-art pieces) could make writing workshop more successful for more students in the long run.

Of course, as you teach any unit, you may decide to devote an extra day to this or that skill. We suggest the units be five weeks and have included only eighteen to twenty sessions, so you will have time for at least five more sessions. The series as a whole provides you with many resources to help you add sessions designed especially for your students, should your assessments reveal additional needs. The cumulative phonics-review materials, available in the online resources, provide suggestions for additional sessions you might teach to support spelling and phonics. If you want to provide more support for a specific skill, such as writing with sensory details or punctuating sentences, you might look through the corresponding unit for a prior grade, studying the lessons on those topics and then adapt them to fit into your unit. You will certainly rely on *Supporting All Writers: High-Leverage Small Groups and Conferences, K–2*, locating small groups that perfectly match your students' needs. You can also alter those groups so they become whole-class teaching. Another option is to invent minilessons yourself that address the skills students need to learn, drawing especially on *Writing Pathways* and on the *Up the Ladder Writing* "Annotated Writing Developed through the Progressions."

Although it is entirely reasonable to plan a detour in your unit of study, I advise strongly against stretching a unit beyond six weeks. At that point, most youngsters would be better served by wrapping up a chunk of work and getting a fresh start on some new work. You, as well as your children, are apt to lose steam if a unit lasts more than five or six weeks, so wrap things up!

Some General Principles to Keep in Mind about Supporting All Learners

When supporting students not yet writing at benchmark levels, the same strategies and accommodations will not work the same way for everyone. As different as every learner is, however, there are some important principles to keep in mind. These apply to working with any learner, but they are especially important when working with students who need the most support.

The Units of Study are designed within the Universal Design for Learning Framework.

Picture the entrance to an older building you know well. Do you see stairs leading to the main entrance, with a ramp around the corner that leads to a side door? Chances are, that building was retrofitted with the best of intentions to make sure that everyone in the community had access. The Universal Design for Learning (UDL) framework helps us see that we can do better. Had the original building been built flush with the ground, two ways to access the building and two entrances wouldn't have been necessary. That is, a better goal for the architects would have been to be design the building, right from the start, with everyone's accessibility in mind.

Putting UDL's Three Principles into Practice with the Units of Study

The Units of Study in Writing are designed with this framework in mind. While UDL has been around and practiced for decades, it has lately been receiving new interest within the recommendations of ESSA. While authoring the units, the coauthors and I thought hard about ways we could design units with accessibility for all as a main goal. We kept in mind the three principles at the heart of UDL: provide multiple means of engagement, provide multiple means of representation, and provide multiple means of action and expression.

For instance, we've focused on building a vibrant classroom community where all students see themselves as readers and writers as a way to reduce fear. We've woven in engaging storylines, as well as relatable stories, as a way to increase interest and relevance, all with the goal of creating motivated learners. We've used consistent language from session to session so that kids know when to key into the most important parts of our teaching. We've written "Ensuring Access" sections for every session to help you separate the essential from the nonessential instruction. We've added visuals and hand gestures across the curriculum to help communicate tricky content. We've detailed powerful work-time supports, so that our teaching is not just about whole-class instruction. And we've suggested varied ways that students can show their learning, based on their strengths. Kids are invited to draw, act out, discuss, and reflect on their writing.

The Relationship between UDL and Differentiated Instruction

For those of you who are less familiar with UDL, it might be tempting to believe that Universal Design for Learning is just a newer term for differentiated instruction. While the two are related, and differentiation firmly belongs within the UDL framework, there are significant differences. For example, UDL most commonly refers to everything from curriculum design to implementation to assessment. It is a mindset that educators take on, aiming to focus on student strengths and to build upon those strengths to reduce or entirely remove instructional obstacles.

When using the UDL framework, educators focus on the big, overarching goals of a unit and lesson. If, for example, the point of a lesson is that writers need to find reasons to support their opinions, whether a student expresses those reasons through role-play, discussion, or drawing is of less importance than the ways in which the teacher is ensuring the student's comprehension of that concept. We've prefaced each session with an "Ensuring Access" section that aims to help you distinguish the essential from the non-essential goals of each session. When the goal is broader than the specific teaching point, the mini-lesson will end with you reminding children of all the optional ways they have before them to engage in the general work of the day. By inviting your children to choose from a repertoire of options, you provide more entry points.

> *As you plan to teach each unit, you will want to hold in mind the strengths and needs of your students.*

Approaching the Minilesson with Accessibility in Mind

As you plan to teach each unit, you will want to hold in mind the strengths and needs of your students. Most lessons and units are designed to be accessible to most students. However, there are times when this will not be the case. Some of this is by design, and some of this is because there are needs the authors of the unit did not anticipate that are present in your classroom. Minilessons tend to fall into one of three main categories:

- **Accessible:** These lessons were written with the UDL Learning Networks in mind. You will notice that there are options for student motivation, a range of pathways to lesson content, and choices for student work and expression of their learning. You can identify these lessons because you will notice right away that there is not much, if anything, you feel compelled to change to give all your learners access. Most of your students, if not all, will experience a high degree of success in these lessons.

- **Accessible with scaffolds:** These lessons are mostly accessible but might require additional scaffolding or adaptations based on your knowledge of your students. For example, you may have students who need support with some of the vocabulary essential to the minilesson. Perhaps a strategy taught that day hinges on an action or movement, such as standing or singing, that will be an obstacle to a student. Or maybe a text used in a minilesson would be traumatic for a member of your class. In these lessons, there might be unanticipated instructional obstacles that only you, with your knowledge of your students, can address.

- **Ambitious:** These lessons are minilessons that set students up for the future by exposing them to bite-sized pieces of content that are ambitious and that all students will not be apt to access in a deep way at this time. The content in these sessions will be revisited later, with more support. These minilessons tend to be "sneak-peek" lessons in which there is no expectation that all students will become proficient in the content; instead, they offer additional challenge for students who are ready for it, and they preview challenging content that will be accessible to all eventually, when that content is needed. These lessons do not need to be overthought but rather approached with a light hand and moved through quickly.

I encourage you and your colleagues to study the Universal Design for Learning framework and then to crack open your upcoming unit, studying the ways the minilessons in that unit are intentionally designed to give all kids access. Once you've identified those parts, especially those which seem most accessible to your students, you'll want to prioritize them as you teach.

Access to curriculum is an important goal.

The objective is always to support all learners in accessing the grade-level curriculum. That means that when planning, you should ask questions, such as, "What will give all students access to this teaching?" You'll want to think, "What might be difficult for certain students about this lesson (or series of lessons)? Is there a way I can remove or adjust it?" and "What will it look like when students do this work?" It also helps to ask, "What content from this unit is essential—and what content is nice but not crucial?" Thinking about these goals can help you improve pathways and prioritize the accommodations you'll need to make.

There are some who suggest that children writing far below grade-level benchmarks should not attend minilessons. They suggest that these students should instead work on word work activities or something of that nature while the rest of the class gathers for the minilesson. These suggestions are based on the notion that certain students are "not ready" and need to fulfill some type of prerequisites before joining their peers. We urge you not to do this for several reasons. The idea that a few students would be segmented from the rest and, perhaps, thus be made to feel that they are not capable enough to attend the whole-class lesson feels problematic. For starters, all students must have access to their grade-level curriculum, and the Units of Study are designed to do exactly that. Also, the minilesson is not just the teaching for that day, it is a community-building experience, one that can help all kids feel part of the intellectual community in your classroom. This kind of social-emotional support is critical. Additionally, as is mentioned elsewhere in this book, the minilesson is designed to be a short instructional piece, allowing students plenty of time to get the individualized and small-group instruction they need during the work time, while also allowing them to understand the greater context and purpose of their learning. Finally, this practice of removing from core instruction those students who are most vulnerable only furthers their vulnerability in making necessary progress. When they are able to rejoin whole-class instruction, they must make up for missed lessons in addition to the current ones, effectively increasing the cognitive load for vulnerable students exponentially.

Boost student access inside minilessons.

There are a number of very effortless ways you can make any minilesson more accessible. Below, I outline a few of these in greater depth.

Assigning Roles within Partnerships

Think for a moment about the typical partnership work that occurs in the midst of minilessons. If partnerships are left on their own, often the same student—usually the more proficient or dominant student—will take the lead. So, if you say, "Turn and tell your partner some reasons we could give for loving this book," and you give just a minute or two for students to talk about this, there often isn't time for both youngsters to talk. Typically, the stronger student does the work, and the less proficient one becomes the sounding board.

Because this is predictable, you can add a layer of support to your minilessons by assigning roles to students within their partnerships. I recommend identifying one student as Partner 1 and the other as Partner 2. You can make a point of asking one or the other to talk or to talk first, alternating this over the course of days. If you assign one member of each partnership to be Partner 1 and the other Partner 2, you might consistently make the more verbal partner be Partner 2. This would allow you to make deliberate decisions, at a particular time, as to whether the more or less verbal partner will talk first. For example, when you ask partners to share ideas for how to end an information book, the first person to be able to offer a thought will probably be in the easier position. On the other hand, there might be times when the person who talks first will have the more challenging role and can provide the less verbal partner with a helpful demonstration.

Embedding Assessments and Coaching Responsively

Another way to make your minilessons more accessible to all is to coach responsively based on your observations. During the active engagement section of every minilesson, you'll channel students to work together to practice what you have just taught. As they do so, listen carefully to ascertain whether they are grasping what you are trying to teach. Then coach in response to what you observe them saying or writing. You might say something like this: "You are describing your insect using very general words. Try

zooming in on just one part of the insect—perhaps just its legs, or just its eyes—and then reach for detailed words to describe that part." Occasionally you'll share the responses of one or two students to serve as a model for others. "Listen to Sabrina's comment and then try to add on to it."

Just a word of caution: the trick is to coach students responsively without extending the minilesson beyond ten minutes in length. You may need to crop portions of the minilesson to stay within that time frame, and you certainly will need to leave many issues to be addressed in small groups or conferences rather than through coaching during the minilesson.

Providing Visual Texts as a Scaffold

Another way to adapt your minilessons so they support all students is to offer visual examples as scaffolding. If a strategy you are teaching includes several steps, you might post a chart listing those steps. During the teaching portion of the minilesson, touch each step on the chart as you demonstrate it, helping students connect your demonstration with the step of the strategy. Then, during the active engagement, you might say something like this: "Remember, I have a chart up here with steps you can follow to do this work. Use it if you need it."

Add illustrations to your charts whenever possible. Illustrations often function to make an abstract concept more concrete and accessible for learners. Study the suggested anchor charts in the online resources for examples of how illustrations can capture complex activities and concepts. Whenever possible, keep your illustrations consistent across charts so that, for example, whenever you ask students to stop and think, you use the same thought bubble.

In *Supporting All Writers: High-Leverage Small Groups and Conferences, K–2*, you'll be given access to all the high-leverage charts and other tools from grade levels preceding your own. Be prepared to draw on those resources to teach kids in such a way that you start where that child is and then take that child as far as you can.

Sharing Student Work Samples that Are Appropriate and Relatable in a Strength-Based Way

Sometimes when teaching writing in minilessons, you will share a sample of student work. Whether this piece of writing is meant to be an exemplar or writing from a peer that students are being asked to "help" with, consider the choice of texts to share. Sometimes this might mean that you group students in the meeting area who have similar strengths and needs to study a piece that most closely resembles their zone of proximal development. Other times, this might mean that when you look to revise or edit another student's work, you select writing that is not out of reach for your students' current writing ability. This will certainly mean you don't always rely on the samples that are highlighted in the Units of Study.

Seating Students Strategically

Seating students strategically can also help boost success during minilessons. Many teachers assign students to spots on the rug, next to their writing partners, and make careful choices about which students to seat in the most easily accessible spots on the rug. If you have a paraprofessional or another colleague in the room during your minilesson, you might suggest that he sit near particular students. Although most children will probably learn easily while sitting on the floor, you may have a few students who will benefit from sitting in a nearby chair. Some will benefit from being given fidgets or stress balls to hold to help them listen.

Drawing On Coteaching Structures Flexibly

If you're fortunate enough to have multiple adults in your room during minilessons, we encourage you to think flexibly about how you draw on coteaching structures as you teach. At times, one adult might teach while the other observes. This method is best when you want to see kids in action and when you want one adult to assess in the midst of teaching. Or one adult might teach while the other assists. You might use a parallel teaching model, splitting the class and having each teacher teaching the same lesson, in the same way, to a smaller group of students. You might rely on station teaching, with each adult in charge of a particular station and providing either intense instruction on a topic or focused coaching to support kids who are writing independently. Or, if the needs of a particular group of students are particularly specialized, you might use an alternative teaching model, where one teacher takes responsibility for teaching the large group and the other works with a smaller group to reteach, enrich, or even preteach a particular concept. Team teaching is also an option, where both teachers lead a lesson together for the whole group.

I detail these particular methods not to suggest that one method is a panacea—it won't be—but to suggest that you have varied methods at your disposal. Rather than fall back on the same method, day in and day out, take a close look at what you are teaching and the needs of your particular students at that time, and choose the methods that will most accelerate students forward.

Student Materials that Increase Writing Access

There are a few materials that you will want to consider when thinking about increasing access to writing workshop for your students:

- **Felt-tip pens or fine-tip markers:** Occupational therapists tell us that the tools we use when writing can make or break volume, stamina, and even our grips. When students are able to write with felt-tip pens or markers, they can reduce the amount of pressure they must exert on their utensil and increase the amount of time they spend writing. Additionally, they learn over time how to self-regulate the amount of pressure needed to form letters since a felt-tip is very unforgiving when too much pressure is applied. A bonus is that not only are felt-tip pens fun to write with, students also can see their writing a little bit better, making it easier to reread, revise, and edit.

- **Extended paper choice:** Paper choice is a hallmark of writing workshop. You will want to offer a range of paper choices for your students, changing the alternatives as units and needs change. Additionally, you might want to include extended paper choice that can offer additional access points, such as one inch or three-quarters of an inch grid paper, paper with raised lines to help modulate letter formation, paper with symbols that guide young writers as to where to start or stop letters, and so on. Some writers report that even the color of the paper can be helpful. Consider light blues and yellows, if you have them available, to help cut down on glare and perhaps even signal different stages of the writing process.

- **Slant boards, standing desks, walls, or floors to write on:** Some writers will benefit from writing surfaces other than the usual desk or tabletop. For students who tend to use their elbows when they write or who have looser grips, writing on a slant board or a wall, or even on the floor while lying on their bellies, can offer full arm and wrist support.

- **Sound wall:** For some students, especially those with print-based difficulties, traditional word walls can be challenging to use. If that is the case for some of your students, you might consider a sound wall. These are walls that post a visual connected to a sound. Below the picture would be listed examples of words that use that sound but might be spelled in a variety of ways. For example, for the sound /sh/, a picture of someone with a finger to her lips might be posted, with the words *machine*, *shout*, and *ocean* under it. For students who are working on their sound and letter connections, sound walls can be a powerful tool to getting words down on paper.

- **Letter charts:** For some students, remembering each letter, both lowercase and uppercase and how to form them, can be a challenge. Offering table- or desk-sized versions of your class charts, especially ones that indicate where the writer should begin to form the letters, can be key tools to creating student writing independence.

- **Digital tablets with primary-friendly composition apps:** While we generally encourage the use of paper and pen or marker for our younger students, there are times when technology can help to reduce or remove obstacles to composition. You might have a student who grapples with remembering his ideas as he writes because the cognitive load of encoding is so much he forgot what he was going to say before finishing the sentence. Or you might have a student who would benefit from being able to hear back what she wrote after recording it. Using an app might be exactly what these students needs. There are many apps available for young writers. Generally speaking, we prefer apps that most closely resemble the paper choices inside the writing workshop classroom and not ones that are too prescriptive. One such app, Book Creator, allows students to record their voices and to use a stylus to draw and write, much as one would use a pen and paper. This allows our young writers to first sketch and then write down their thoughts, either before or after they create an audio recording of those thoughts.

A Word about Teacher or Adult Transcription

It can be tempting to step in when a student is struggling mightily with getting words down on paper or when either you or the child finds the youngster's own writing hard to read. I encourage you, however, to avoid doing this. It can make a young writer feel dependent, as if she can only write when an adult is on hand to transcribe. If you really want to provide transcription services, help the child use a dictation or voice app, or ask the child to write as usual and then record her voice, reading what she's written aloud. That recording can be stored in a QR code.

Stay focused on students' individual goals and on ways you are helping them make progress toward those goals.

When you are deciding what to prioritize, begin by focusing on goals for a student, which should be included in an IEP if the student has one. For example, if a primary goal for a student is to express herself more and to increase her participation in class conversations, then you or another adult might preview selected minilessons and read-alouds with this student, helping her think about what she could say to participate. If that student works with an adult volunteer during breakfast twice a week, you might ask the volunteer to read parts of that day's anchor charts or mentor texts to the child and to converse with her, setting her up to feel more confident in class. In this example, my goal was not for the child to master the content of the lesson but rather to feel confident enough to participate. When you have clear goals for students, you can more easily ensure that the help you provide is aligned to those goals. The learner will be more apt to make observable progress. Setting achievable and important goals and helping learners see themselves meeting those goals can turn around your children's learning curves.

As you set goals for students, think about the intersection of IEP goals and unit-based goals. IEP goals are often long term, something students are working on across a year. It's helpful if students also have short-term goals within a unit of study that will help them work toward those long-term goals. You might ask, "What could be a unit-based goal that intersects with this reader's IEP goal?" For instance, if a child's IEP goal is to write a narrative story in sequential order on a second-grade level, a short-term goal might be for the student to quickly say, sketch, or write a sequenced story, touching and telling each part from the beginning to the end, before starting to write. If this is the short-term goal, think about ways you might see evidence of the child making progress toward that goal. Perhaps you'll pull up alongside the writer in the midst of writing and ask the youngster to go back and touch and tell the story to you.

It is helpful to identify key times for checking in around particular goals, based on the sequence of the unit. So, you might jot into your unit book that after Bend II, you want to check on four kids' work toward particular goals.

Prioritize teaching toward independence.

It is true that there are endless things you could do to support learners. You could cover the feet of your chairs in cut-out tennis balls to minimize any undue background noise. You could create goal sheets for every lesson. You could make graphic organizers for half of the sessions. You could enlarge every text and also make individual pocket-size copies of it. The hard truth is that there are a thousand things you could do for each of your students, but not a thousand hours in the day.

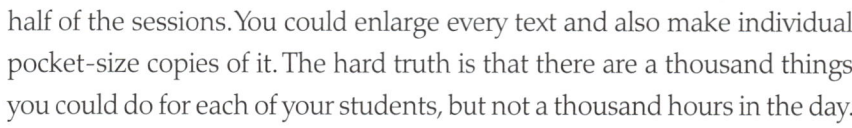

Prioritizing the supports for your learners is important. This means that some days you will offer more support to some groups or individuals than others. But I want to caution you against spending endless hours developing materials so that each child is always being given a new scaffold. In some cases, a particular graphic organizer may be useful, but too many can be overwhelming. Certainly, if you do introduce a scaffold, introduce it as a temporary scaffold, saying, "I'm giving you this chart now to help you try different ways of labeling your writing. In two weeks, you'll be able to do this labeling without the support of this tool." Make it clear to students from the onset that the ultimate goal is for them to work independently.

I worry that too often, with the best of intentions in mind, we surround our writers who need support with so much help that they never get opportunities to work with independence. It's critical that all students have opportunities to work with independence, to the extent that they are able, and that they have this opportunity at school. Predictable structures will go a long way in ensuring that all kids can work with independence.

> *The hard truth is that there are a thousand things you could do for each of your students, but not a thousand hours in the day.*

That said, I want to be clear here: I am speaking only about the day-to-day adjustments and scaffolds we offer students to give them the support they need to be as independent as possible. These you will want to pick and choose as needed, but when a student has particular accommodations on an IEP, you will want to be mindful of those and ensure that those are always available when appropriate.

Supporting Writers with Learning Disabilities

Identifying and Supporting Students with Dyslexia

Since dyslexia is the most commonly identified learning disability, it feels critical to devote space to discussing the relationship between students diagnosed with dyslexia and the writing workshop. We believe that the writing workshop—with its structural flexibility and focus on meeting the needs of individual learners during work time through conferences, small-group work, and differentiated materials while concurrently offering access to grade-level curriculum during minilessons—can be easily adapted to meet the needs of students who have dyslexia. While reading is the activity where people with this learning profile will face the most challenges, this is followed in close and sometimes more clear succession by writing. We agree with Maryanne Wolf, Director of the UCLA Center for Dyslexia, Diverse Learners and Social Justice, who says that the child with dyslexia also comes with beautiful assets that can shine when given the opportunity. We believe that allowing children to share is especially possible within the workshop structure.

That said, for this to happen, you, and ideally your school, must be mindful of instructional choices that will allow your workshop to work. It is incredibly easy to assume that dyslexia needs to be addressed only when it comes to reading, phonemic awareness, and phonics. However, writing is the exhale of reading, to borrow a phrase, and can pose unique obstacles for those with dyslexia. Additionally, and perhaps even more importantly, writing gives a rich and purposeful reason for students to have regular and predictable practice of those ever-important phonics skills.

We recommend that students be screened for dyslexia, especially in kindergarten and grade 1 (and in fact, many states require this). We have not included screeners for dyslexia within this curriculum since different districts and states rely on different tools. You'll want to check with your district about which tools you should use and the recommended timeline for screening students.

It is important to keep in mind that you cannot use a screener to diagnose a child with dyslexia. Only doctors can do that. An official diagnosis requires a formal evaluation, with a battery of clinical assessments. As a result, some kids with this disability will be undiagnosed. Therefore, it is especially important for you to be aware of common indicators of dyslexia so that you can monitor for these and possibly follow up to find out more information.

Common Dyslexia Indicators

- Trouble with rhyme

- Trouble associating sound with symbols

- Difficulty with word retrieval when talking, which may result in frustration

- Difficulty following simple or complex directions

- Difficulty spelling

- Difficulty with writing with volume

- Difficulty breaking simple words, such as *sit*, *pup*, *nap*, into individual sounds

- Errors in reading based on pictures or context, with little or no attention to the letters and their sounds on the page (reading *bath* instead of *tub*)

- Frustration expressed or avoidance displayed during reading activities

Children with dyslexia need especially intensive phonics instruction.

Students with dyslexia need intensive, systematic, sequential instruction in phonemic awareness and phonics. These students need each phoneme, morpheme, grapheme, and so on to be explicitly taught. These students benefit from discrete, incremental, and repetitive instruction for phonological concepts. Most interventions for dyslexia focus primarily on the phonological and phonics components in reading, so you'll want to be sure that the phonics education these children receive is transferred into the writing workshop—and that will probably rest on your shoulders.

These students will need you to clearly teach them how to transfer their knowledge of phonics into their writing. You can provide that instruction within your writing workshop. So, even if, and especially when, a child might be in a separate location for phonics instruction, you will want to advocate for the child to still participate in your writing workshop. Chances are good that you'll have some students who do not have a dyslexia diagnosis but who's writing instruction could be tweaked so it especially supports phonemic awareness and phonics.

No matter how your students receive their systematic, sequential phonics and phonemic awareness instruction, close communication between you and other teachers is especially critical for students with dyslexia. They benefit from aligned instruction, with consistent strategies and techniques, and from prompting in which adults use the same cues across their literacy instruction. This alignment in instruction both reduces the cognitive load of receiving disparate messages and increases the opportunities for repetition and transference. You and your colleagues will want to develop a system for communicating what has been taught, any mnemonics tools or prompts that can be relied upon, and places where each of you is shifting toward more student independence in a particular skill.

High-Frequency Word Practice

Students with dyslexia may also need more support when it comes to learning to write snap words. While students without dyslexia may be able to orthographically map and recall a sight word after two to four repetitions, students with dyslexia often need to orthographically map a word twenty to forty times and may need as many as sixty repetitions. The challenge is to make these practices joyful rather than tedious. To support you, we've included work times across the units that are filled with joyful, often multisensory, ways kids can practice words repeatedly. While snap words are addressed extensively and often in your phonics and reading workshop units, we believe that it is in writing workshop where they truly become solidified. If you notice that your students are not developing the word-writing automaticity you would hope, you might study their time spent in writing workshop. Are they often pulled from writing workshop or otherwise interrupted during that time? While we agree that writing workshop is often an ideal time for push-in services or interventions, we also want to keep a close eye on students' independent time to ensure they have plenty of opportunity to solidify their new learning by practicing it in writing workshop.

It's important to acknowledge and celebrate the strengths that students with dyslexia bring to the classroom. These students are often among our deepest and most creative thinkers. They are the ones who knock our socks off when we have brainstorming sessions to share new writing ideas. They are often the ones who serve as class problem solvers, looking at puzzling quandaries in unique ways. The creative minds and deep empathy that are common in students with these learning profiles can and often do bring an invaluable level of depth and warmth to our classrooms. We encourage you to capitalize on these strengths by providing your students with plenty of opportunity for grand conversations as part of read-aloud and independent reading work.

> *It's important to acknowledge and celebrate the strengths that students with dyslexia bring to the classroom. These students are often among our deepest and most creative thinkers.*

For more information, we recommend *Overcoming Dyslexia: Second Edition* by Sally Shaywitz, M.D.

Other Writing Difficulties to Consider

Because the act of writing is so transparent, it is often where students who have academic difficulties or perhaps learning disabilities are discovered. While it may be true that some people have a real talent for writing, we believe wholeheartedly that writing is a skill that can be taught.

However, students with various learning profiles, including dyslexia, may find writing more challenging. We list a few of these profiles here—knowing that this is by no means a comprehensive list—to give you some insights that will help you to consider possible needs your students have and to enlist the expertise of your administrator or learning specialist team for further support.

- **Dysgraphia:** This was once listed in the Diagnostic and Statistical Manual of Mental Disorders but is no longer considered a disability. It refers to a person's specific difficulty in writing and might involve letter formation, spacing between words, spelling, grammar, or just legibility. While dysgraphia is no longer considered a disability on its own, some students might simply have difficulties with the mechanics of writing and not the composition, organization, and craft of it. These students benefit from explicit instruction for those mechanics, as well as the occasional use of digital tools in the primary grades.

- **Written expression disorder:** This disorder is different from dysgraphia, which mostly deals with the mechanics of writing. People with written expression disorder have a difficult time getting their thoughts on paper. They can often tell a great story or teach others about information they know verbally, but when it comes time to record those thoughts on paper, they have great difficulty. Their writing may be disorganized; have missing, overused, and confusing words and phrases; and be overall difficult to understand. These students benefit from step-by-step writing instruction, often using paper choice, graphic organizers, and extra support in moving from verbal rehearsal and recording of those thoughts.

The Keys to Ensuring Access for All Learners

Collaborate and communicate with other invested adults.

Too often, the invested adults in a child's life don't talk together about the instruction they are providing for that student. That is, the reading intervention specialist has one goal and pathway for instruction, you have another, the speech therapist a third. Meanwhile, the parent may be actively supporting another path entirely. The result is that the child ends up feeling scattered. Be sure that all service providers talk together about their goals and about ways to help the child meet those goals. This matters tremendously, and the time for these meetings should be prioritized in the school schedule. Service providers are invaluable to both the student and the classroom teacher. For a child to receive cohesive, integrated support, it is crucial that the classroom teacher, service providers, and parents/guardians are all on the same page. This will also mean making sure that service providers can attend professional development to learn more about workshop teaching and about upcoming units of study. You and other classroom teachers will also benefit from attending professional development designed for service providers, so you learn about intervention programs from your more knowledgeable colleagues.

Know what resources are available to you for support.

It is a Herculean task to support all learners—a task that changes from year to year, class to class, and child to child. My respect for you is enormous. I hope that you will find the resources provided in these Units of Study helpful to you as you work to support all your students in accessing the curriculum.

Lean on the *Writing Pathways* and *Supporting All Writers: High-Leverage Small Groups and Conferences, K–2* for support. You'll want to assess your students' needs and plan instruction by drawing on all the resources available. The Units of Study themselves are filled with examples of small-group instruction and conferring to offer support and enrichment, as well as coaching notes for how to adjust the teaching of certain lessons, if needed.

In addition to the Units of Study, there are other helpful resources and materials. Two books that I recommend are *Universal Design for Learning in the Classroom*, edited by Tracey Hall, Anne Meyer, and David Rose, and *Writing Better* by Steve Graham and Karen Harris. And, of course, remember that you and your colleagues are each other's greatest resources. When instruction is aligned across grades, whole-school conversations around writing instruction are possible. Your colleagues are treasure troves of information, and I highly encourage schools to make time, not only for grade-level teams to meet and plan, but also for cross-grade teams to meet and share tips, ideas, insights, and resources.

Index

Moll, Luis, 88
multilingual language learners (MLLs)
   assessments, 89
   identifying strengths of, 88
   getting to know as individuals, 88–89
   helping with figurative language, 101
   identifying strengths of, 88
   including in the classroom community, 93
   introducing to grammar and parts of
      speech, 97–98, 101–2
   minilessons, 94
   predictable classroom structures for, 92–95
   scaffolding, 99–100
   Spanish language previews, translations,
      and texts, 3, 5, 89–92
   using consistent language with, 93–95
   using visuals and gestures with, 95–96
   vocabulary building, 99
   working with language specialists, 102
Multi-Tiered System of Support (MTSS),
    114–15
Murray, Donald, 19, 50

names, identifying writing with, 28
narrative writing development, K–6
    trajectory, 18
no question zone, 31

omitting/adding letters in words, 109
one-day charts, 3, 95
one-to-one conferences, 3. *See also*
    conferring
opinion/argument checklist, 108
orthographical word mapping, 7

paper
   page structure as writing strategy, 37–38
   supplying multiple varieties and options,
     126
partnerships
   assigning roles in, 123
   guiding work of during minilessons, 50
   importance, 20
   managing, 35
   for MLLs, 96–97
   as small groups, 75, 78
   triads, for early language learners, 93
part of the writing process, 23
parts of speech, instruction in, 101
Pearson, David, 4
pencils/pens, 39, 108. *See also* provisioning
    writing workshop; writing tools
phonics awareness
   for dyslexic students, 130–31

   teaching alongside Units of Study, 8
   transferring to writing, 6
   using writing to enhance, 6
phonological awareness, 6–7
play activities, pretending, learning through,
    6
prior knowledge, referencing and extending,
    6–7, 80
"private offices," 35
professional development
   collaborative learning communities, 74
   importance, 4, 118, 132–33
   learning from colleagues/mentors, 5,
     44–45, 69
   and MTSS/RTI, 114
Proulx, Annie, 40
provisioning writing workshop. *See also*
    mentor texts
   papers and folders, 37–38
   sticky notes, 37, 70–71, 77, 81
   writing utensils, revision tools, 8, 37, 39, 68,
     108, 126
publishing, 13, 22–24. *See also* mentor texts
punctuation, focusing on, 6, 23, 79, 98, 101

rally portion (small groups), 80
recapping
   earlier learning, 46–47, 82
   minilesson teaching point, 35, 48
   overheard conversations, 45
record-keeping, following conferences,
    70–71
Reeves, Doug, 110
rehearsing writing, 21, 90
rereading
   by early writers, 27
   importance, 40
   as an initial daily activity, 28
   during minilessons, 50
research portion (conferences)
   goal, 61–62
   helping writers articulate intentions,
     60–61
   initial review of writer's work, 59
   using multiple lines of questioning,
     61–62
revising
   coaching prompts, 76–77
   as part of the writing process, 21, 23
   for readability, small group example,
     76–77
   revision tools, 39
   small group coaching for, 76
Rose, David, 133